The Museum of
Modern Art, Gunma

Phaidon Press Ltd
Regent's Wharf
All Saints Street
London N1 9PA

First published 1996

© 1996 Phaidon Press Limited

Photographs © 1996
Yasuhiro Ishimoto

ISBN 0 7148 3549 8

A CIP catalogue record for
this book is available from the
British Library.

Printed in Singapore

The Museum of Modern Art, Gunma

Arata Isozaki

Philip Drew
ARCHITECTURE IN DETAIL

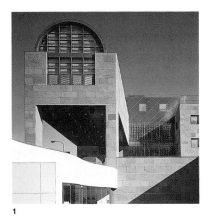

Arata Isozaki's work is known and admired on an international scale. Outside Japan, Isozaki is responsible for a number of brilliant projects, the most outstanding being the Museum of Contemporary Art in Los Angeles (1981–86), the Brooklyn Museum and the Palladium Club in New York (1983–85). More recently, Isozaki completed the Team Disney Headquarters by Lake Buena Vista in Florida. Across the Atlantic in Spain he designed a Sports Hall for the 1992 Olympics sited on Montjuic, Barcelona, from which arose the sports pavilion at Palafolls. While each of these buildings is outstanding on its own terms, the Museum of Modern Art in the Japanese prefecture of Gunma remains his magnum opus, a work of such all-embracing artistic stature that even today, twenty years later, it stands unchallenged as the single most encompassing summary of Isozaki's architectural thinking and achievements.

The museum was completed in 1974, a little over ten years after Isozaki founded his own independent architectural practice in 1963. Its design brought to a climax an intense conceptual phase which Isozaki abandoned soon afterwards. For this reason, the museum's significance has grown rather than diminished with the passing years. It took on board more completely than any previous – and, in retrospect, later – work a fundamental artistic premise that continues in Isozaki's work, but never in quite such an over-arching or single-minded fashion. There have been many detours in Isozaki's career to visit interesting architectural territory – indeed, so many that it is impossible at times to differentiate the passing from the enduring strands. The Museum of Modern Art,

Gunma is the most complete realization by Isozaki of a conceptual architectural approach which is never entirely absent from his later work. The museum's cubic thesis had its roots in the earlier Oita Prefectural Library and Nakayama House of 1964,[1] and it recently resurfaced in the New Oita Prefectural Library (1994). Subsequent designs have elaborated parts of the original Gunma Museum scheme, giving prominence to some aspects at the expense of others. Thus the quickest and most thorough introduction to Isozaki's architecture is a visit to the Gunma Museum. Most of his architectural thinking is embodied in it in one form or another – not everything by any means, but enough, to the extent that to miss Gunma is to risk not understanding Isozaki at all, at least the early mature Isozaki of the 1960s and 1970s. Although so much has happened since in his work, the Gunma Museum, along with the first Oita Library, are the best and most reliable pointers to Arata Isozaki's future career as well as his two most important early works. They are also extraordinarily compelling architectural achievements.

A slice of genuine Japan The Museum of Modern Art, Gunma is located near Takasaki, a medium-sized provincial city 125 km (78 miles) northwest of Tokyo. Bruno Taut described Takasaki as 'garishly provincial' during his stay there sixty years ago.[2] Taut later added that it was among its farmers that he discovered, 'a deep simplicity and naturalness more powerful than any dull reflection of the Kyoto culture.'[3] Takasaki is well situated

1 The Museum of Contemporary Art, Los Angeles, 1981–86, view of elevated pavilion above the entrance and the copper-sheathed barrel-vaulted bridge which forms a gateway to the museum.
2 The Disney Building, Lake Buena Vista, Florida, 1987–90, view from the northwest across the lake of the long office wing broken in the middle by the entry core.
3 Interior view of the New Oita Prefectural Library, Oita, 1994.

4

4 Oita Prefectural Library, Oita, 1962–66, west elevation. Isozaki's obsession with square sections and cubes first revealed itself in the 1964 Nakayama House, Oita (now demolished) and this library.
5 New Oita Prefectural Library, Oita, 1994.
6 The abandoned park for army munitions storage was overgrown with a thick cover of trees and dense undergrowth; this was penetrated by an east–west spine road which supplied the leading vertebral axis for Isozaki in his arrangement of the Gunma composition. The photograph shows the spine access road prior to development.

5

in the southeast of Gunma Prefecture, a generally mountainous region, save for a small area where the upland drops onto the northern edge of the broad Kanto plain in which the city stands.

Takasaki is certainly a provincial city, but Taut was guilty of exaggeration. Gunma Prefecture is considered to be the birthplace of Eastern Japan; it was here that early clay Haniwa pottery figures were unearthed which, along with the presence of more than 8,000 ancient burial mounds, attest to the early date of advanced culture in the region.[4] Today, the prefecture is rapidly assuming many of the characteristics of a suburb of Tokyo with the northward expansion of chemical, electrical and machine industries from the Keihin Industrial Zone. The prefecture is furthermore famous for politicians such as Yasuhiro Nakasone, the son of a wealthy timber merchant, who served as the country's Prime Minister from 1982–87.[5]

The Museum of Modern Art is ten minutes by taxi east of Takasaki in Gunma-no-mori Park, on the opposite side of the city to Shorinzan where Bruno Taut lived from 1933–36 in a little house in the grounds of the Daruma Temple.[6] The park is large, containing 25 hectares, much of it densely treed.

Taut's characterization of Japanese life and its architectural culture greatly influenced European and American perceptions of Japan, notably his claim that Katsura Imperial Villa was the finest example of a pure Japanese aesthetic and his rejection of the sumptuous Toshogu Shrine at Nikko.[7] In addition, he made a deep impression on the Japanese. Fusaichiro Inoue, for example, who had helped prepare Taut's house in 1933 for the German architect's stay at Takasaki,[8] was later to become the driving force behind the establishment of an art museum in Gunma Prefecture. Inoue had acquired a record over many years of supporting innovative architectural projects, and it was Inoue who commissioned Antonin Raymond to design the Gunma Music Centre for Takasaki (1961) to house the Gunma Symphony Orchestra, Japan's first citizens' orchestra. Antonin Raymond adopted a novel concrete folded-plate fireproof construction throughout to resist seismic forces which saved money, then in short supply – a factor that also affected the Gunma Museum of Modern Art.

The search for a plan Gunma-no-mori Park was established to commemorate the centenary of the Meiji uprising which had restored the emperor to power in 1868. Prior to this the park had been used to store army munitions, but after the war it was no longer required for this purpose and many of the buildings, including the army ammunition storage bunkers, fell into disrepair and ruin. The ammunition storage facility was located away from Takasaki to protect the city from the danger of an explosion. Indeed, Maebashi, not Takasaki, is the capital of Gunma Prefecture; however, the possibility of conflict over the museum's location was avoided since it was outside Takasaki, in between the two cities.

The initiative to create a museum inside the park took shape slowly and only really gained momentum after the 1968 centenary. In 1970, a first step was taken with the setting up of a museum committee consisting of

6

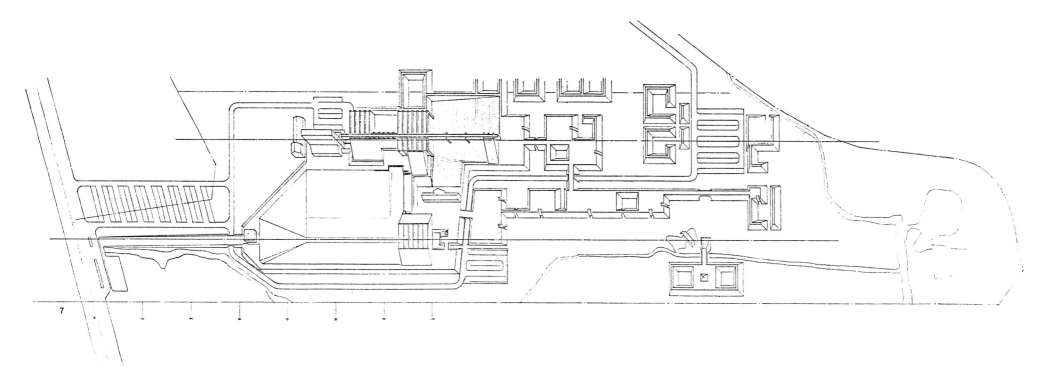

6 Mr Kanda, Prefectural Governor, and Fusaichiro Inoue from Takasaki who was already well known for his support of the arts. The committee consulted Fumihiko Maki, Masato Otaka and Arata Isozaki – all of them young architects at the beginning of their careers. Maki and Otaka already knew each other from their Metabolism days when they had worked jointly on Generic Group Form and space studies, notably their Shinjuku Redevelopment Project.[9] Isozaki had recently reached the end of his involvement on the Festival Plaza at Expo 70, Osaka, but at that time he was still relatively little known to the Japanese public at large. The committee's instructions to the three architects were to produce a rough conceptual plan for the 25 hectare park site. It was in this manner that the siting of the present Museum of Modern Art at the western end of the park was decided.

Gumna-no-mori Park is a long rectangular-shaped strip of level land running east–west. A watercourse crossed its southwestern tip and there were two pronounced depressions at the eastern end. The eastern half was crowded with rectangular earth berms around the obsolete wartime explosives stores which had an elaborate system of roads for access. By 1971 the park had become overgrown with a thick cover of trees and dense undergrowth. Several abandoned industrial buildings remained at the northwest sector, and an east–west road, which formed a linear spine, ran the length of the park. Because the site is pinched on its western boundary the entry to the proposed museum was restricted to the southwest corner closest to Takasaki.

Maki, Otaka and Isozaki initially dispersed the museum in pavilions over the entire site of the park. This changed, however, after Arata Isozaki was appointed sole architect for the art museum in November 1971 and the museum committee was re-formed; its members included Fusaichiro Inoue representing the local community of Takasaki, Teiichi Hijikata, Director of the Kanagawa Prefectural Museum of Modern Art designed by Junzo Sakakura, and Mr Kawakita, the Director of the Kyoto Museum of Modern Art. Their role was to supervise the new museum's design development.[10] Inoue had for a long time been trying to convince the prefecture that it needed an art museum. In fact, he was so determined that, frustrated by a lack of funds early on in the project, he established a gallery in his own office as a temporary measure. Only then was the idea of a prefectural art museum finally accepted. Even so, the prefecture was forced to borrow additional money from banks – a common practice by Japanese local government – to cover the final cost of the work.

Isozaki made a rapid start on Gunma in February 1971 and by April he had produced four alternative design studies. This was the first of many reports; there were four in all before a final design was achieved at the end of March 1972,[11] although, even then, design development continued through to September. The most intense period, during which the cubic form with the museum space wedged between two wings at either end and an angled standing pavilion emerged, occurred in the months following October 1971 and extended through to the end of January 1972. The range of solutions canvassed in these schematics testify to the intensity of

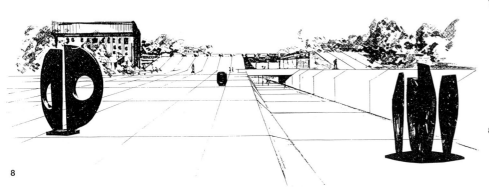

7 Aerial view of Schematic Design I (March 1971) based on an extended guitar-like body using the existing blast-deflection mounds to create a series of mastabas and roof platforms, and tied into an existing industrial structure at the western end of the site.

8 Schematic Design I, perspective from the plaza the surface of which is continued up over the art gallery. On the east, a water channel provides access to the buried entry.

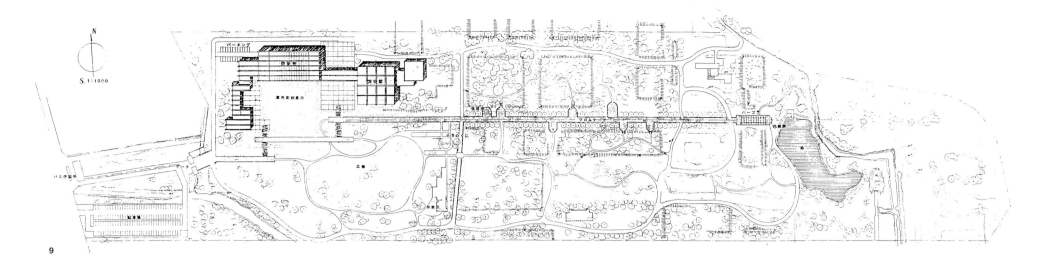

9

Isozaki's search and eagerness to consider every available option. The first series is particularly interesting since, little by little, the final museum concept begins to emerge, at first hesitantly, then with great clarity early in 1972.

In March 1971 Isozaki produced Schematic Design I in which an extended linear shaped guitar-like form was married to mastaba-like earth berms and platforms using the existing blast-deflection mounds.[12] These earth forms were overlaid by the tree canopy. This subsequently led Isozaki to formulate a concept of transparent cubes through which the trees in the park would be visible.

The idea of physically expressing the conceptual framework, and the landscape impulse which emerged alongside it early in the schematic design stage, supplies an important insight into the origins of the visually transparent *parti* for the later formal cubic arrangement. At this point, Isozaki intended to sink the museum buildings into the earth. His sections indicate an art museum partly buried with its roof, much like the inclined roof of his design for the Oita branch of the Fukuoka Bank, rising from the surrounding ground of the park. In a perspective,[13] Isozaki introduced a sunken channel at right angles to the museum; the museum's wall slopes up from a large plaza beside it and an existing industrial structure is tied into the east–west axis of the building. The roof of the museum is treated as a series of closely-spaced transverse beams reminiscent of those at the Oita Library. Although the idea of a visually transparent structure of cubes did not arise until some time later, and the connection may even seem tenuous, the intention to reflect the green from the landscape emerges early on in the project and is a continuing preoccupation for Isozaki, and appears in all the subsequent sketches to varying degrees.

Schematic Design II introduced a single-storey arrangement of pavilions with exposed roof beams which stepped around the northwest corner of the site and coalesced in a large rectangular-shaped mass subdivided into sixteen square modules in the east.[14] This sketch showed an art museum connected to the eastern kidney-shaped lake by an long pedestrian spine that began in the lawn in front of the museum. Two short parallel over-lapping paths delivered the park visitor to the southwestern park entrance.

A similar proposal made its appearance in option 'A' of four alternatives (Schematic Design I-1).[15] Type-A was a dispersed arrangement of individual single-storey pavilions,[16] in the main spread out over the northwest corner of the park and interconnected by covered walkways similar to Jørgen Bo and Vilhelm Wohlert's Louisiana Museum at Humlebaek, Denmark (1958). As at Louisiana, Isozaki's beams supporting the flat roofs are part of the architectural expression and run the length of the museum.

The types-B and -C are intermediate designs that lie somewhere between the dispersed Type-A and the compact Type-D schemes. The rectangular pavilions of the second proposal are arranged in casual irregular compositions based on stepped overlapping plan shapes much like the first scheme, but now the smaller pavilions

10

9 Schematic Design II (June 1971). The form is still a tripartite arrangement of a cubic east block separated by a series of staggered pavilions with the entrance between the two. The roof of the pavilions is expressed as a rhythmic series of exposed beams.

10 Aerial view of the model, Schematic Design I-2, Type-A.

11 Louisiana Museum, Humlebaek, Denmark, 1958 by Jørgen Bo and Vilhelm Wohlert. Isozaki's early schemes were inspired by the Louisiana Museum's dispersed arrangement of individual single-storey pavilions which form a continuous walkway around the edge of a garden facing Øre Sound.

11

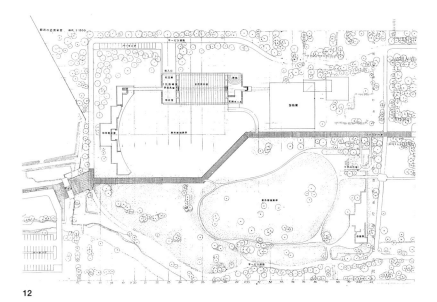

12

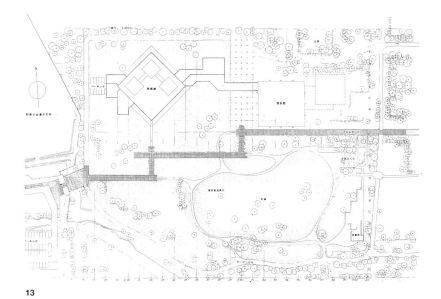

13

have been consolidated into larger units and the roof beams switched around to run longitudinally. The linear rhythm of east–west beams was exploited to unite the individual forms in a pervasive rhythm including a large two-storey gallery space which separated the two ends of the art museum, one cubic mass on the east, and a second, made up of a number of fused terraced galleries grouped around a lawn. The two sections were tied together by a flying bridge at the rear.

In Type-C,[17] the process of consolidation was taken a step further, the western terraced pavilions were eliminated and the museum reduced to a simple rectangle so it straddled an east–west circulation spine between the car park to the west and the future history museum to the east. The block was overlaid by north–south roof beams. Inside the two-storeyed rectangle, the space was simply divided with enclosed squares attached on either side of the spine colonnade. This third scheme returned to the earlier guitar-like *parti* but on this occasion it was more controlled and rational than the later version.

The Type-D solution in the series I-1 was consolidated in a simple inclusive rectangle; two dual-membrane walls separated the main exhibition gallery in the centre from a theatre and entry at the east end and the administration and storage at the other. A vertical stepped pavilion provided a visual terminus to the east–west pedestrian spine. Each of these types was developed further in the subsequent second Schematic Design I-1 series until a point was reached where they either metamorphosed into something entirely new or were dropped. Thus, the D-type[18] became more vertical until it assumed a precise diamond base two storeys high with three cubes mounted on it which had galleries projecting out from the inside surfaces at different levels, connected to one another by flying bridges. In this scheme, the site area called for a building four storeys high with the curatorial functions and public areas contained in the base and exhibition spaces above it. By July 1971 the concept was still in its preliminary stages.

At this juncture, the National Government, which had the responsibility for planning the entire park, intervened to the effect that the Prefectural building programme was confined to a small section of the park. This ruled out the more dispersed concept with buildings connected by covered walkways which Isozaki had been exploring, and automatically ensured that the siting of the projected museum would be in its present location along the northern boundary at the western end of the park.

With the dispersed schemes ruled out, Isozaki concentrated his energies on finding a more compact design. At the same time, he began to think that even with the site so limited in extent, the surrounding trees were still of importance, thus the museum building would continue to borrow the green from its environment. In the second Schematic Design I-2 sketches the four basic approaches, A, B, C and D, were further developed from the first series along with the idea of a museum that was a nearly invisible composition of pure geometric forms through which the landscape can clearly be seen.

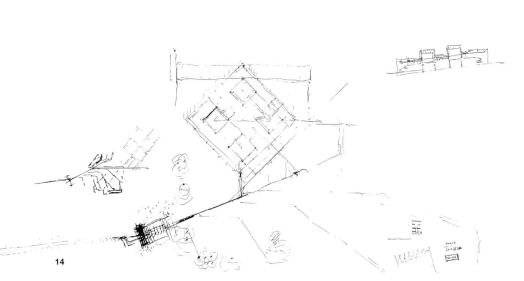

14

15

12 Schematic Design I-1, Type D (June 1971) consolidated the museum into a simple rectangle consisting of double walls and a semicircular fronted stepped pavilion.

13 Schematic Design I-2, Type-D (July 1971) assumed a precise diamond two-storey cube with three cubes mounted inside connected flying bridges.

14 Schematic Design I-2 (July 1971) explores the conceptual basis of cubes within the larger cube.

15 Model of Schematic Design I-2, Type-C (October 1971) was based on a linear east–west circulation spine with galleries attached to both sides, and the administration in a separate block at the eastern end.

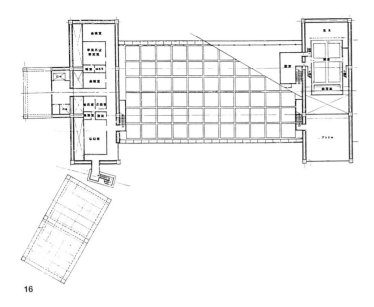

16

16 Plan, Schematic Design II-1
(October 1971). By October
1971 the outline of the final
scheme has begun to emerge,
although it is still very sketchy.

17 Schematic Design II-2, Type-B
(October 1971). This scheme
doubled the thickness of the east
entry block.

18 Schematic Design III-3 (January
1972), plan.

19 Schematic Design III-3 (January
1972), section through the
temporary exhibitions space with
the permanent exhibition gallery
on the upper first floor level
showing the concealed daylight
sources in raised skylight boxes
on the roof.

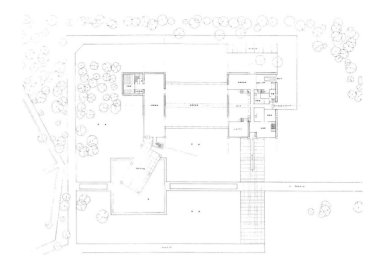

17

First steps The formal design phase ended in September 1972 and construction of the museum began in October of the same year. It was completed in March 1974 in the relatively short time of two-and-a-half years. A discussion of all sixteen later schematic designs is less important than considering the emergent themes. One such idea involved the park and how best to connect the art museum to the main east–west pedestrian spine which had to be deflected south at its western terminus if it was to join the western entrance. Isozaki also asked whether there was some typical form for the contemporary art museum: Is it best expressed as an irregular series of linked galleries? Or is it more typically concerned with art displayed flexibly within a simple geometric envelope?

By October 1971, in the second Schematic Design II-1 series,[19] an embryonic outline emerged but it was still extremely sketchy. At this stage, the art museum consisted of a large rectangular exhibition space between two bookends with a wing allocated to Japanese art already angled towards the park entrance. The point of entry for the public was established in the end east block via a glazed screen and proceeded up a monumental staircase in two flights that led irrevocably to a mezzanine. The later cubic theme was anticipated in the Japanese gallery. From this beginning, a variety of cubic compositions was investigated. The use of large cubes in the composition was confined in the main to the east and west end pavilions. For a while, just one row of cubes was used for the east wing but in Schematic Design II-2 Type-B two equal rows made up of three cubes were introduced at the east end. A long ramp pierced the gap. In most later sketch designs an asymmetrical form was preferred with the inner or western row of cubes substantially longer. This persisted until Schematic Design III-3 in mid-January 1972 when Isozaki again made the rows equal and symmetrical. The location of the lecture theatre proved something of a problem, and Isozaki moved it from the outer east side where it occupied two 12 m² modules so that it straddled both rows of cubes crosswise blocking the important transverse spatial gap running through between the rows.

Surprisingly, because the scheme was still very fluid early in 1972, a design was published in the January 1972 issue of the the magazine *Architecture and Urbanism* (*A+U*). This consisted of a main one-storey exhibition space with a square gridded transparent roof and transparent facades wedged between two north–south blocks; there was a four-cube wing on the east end containing the main entry and gallery administration offices, balanced on the west by a T-shaped block made up of three large cubes with a fourth glued on the outside for storing paintings and containing a stair and goods lift. In front was a separate two-cube gallery hinged at a staircase so it rotated 22½ degrees and pointed towards the southwest entrance of the park. This stood on six stubby pilotis. The tilted gallery was open underneath at the ground level and stood in a square reflecting pond tied to the east–west pedestrian spine leading eastward across the park. The glazed faces of each cube were subdivided by a six-by-six square grid into thirty-six equal panels.

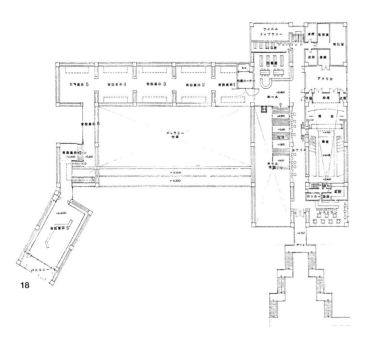

18

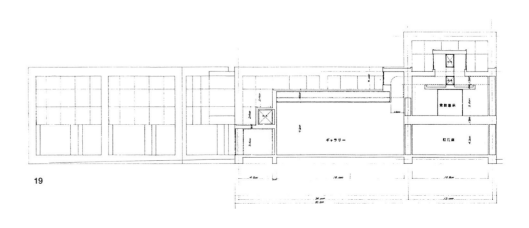

19

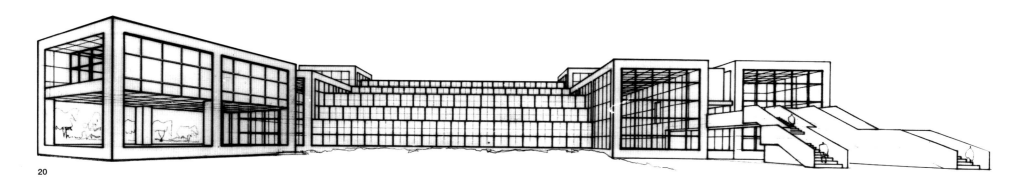

20

In the October 1971 sketches a narrow longitudinal bridge swung across the main exhibition space from east to west at second floor level and divided it into two equal parts thereby establishing a symmetrical spine linking the two sides. On the outside, the gallery profile rose in steps towards the rear. This was abandoned a month later and replaced by art storage behind the first floor Temporary Exhibitions Gallery which served as a platform for the second floor Permanent Exhibitions Gallery, necessitating a stepped section from the front towards the back. There was no thought of an open framework made up of cubes for the Temporary Exhibitions Gallery at this stage, which instead was expressed as a homogeneous transparent grid-surface rising in three tiers. Although the cubic module was respected, the middle section was treated as a plastic unit joining two strong bookends whose purpose seemed to be to hold the centre upright.

The main entrance was through the southernmost cube. This was alternately shown as open with no fenestration, or infilled above the second floor level to match the Japanese gallery to the west. At this stage, Isozaki envisaged the main Temporary Exhibitions Gallery as a simple orthogonal space covered by a grid over every surface with the exhibits freely arranged in De Stijl fashion around the floor in a standard rectangular grid. By mid-February 1972 this was abandoned in favour of a flexible system of rails across the hall suspended from the ceiling.

The principal difference between this proposal and the scheme which was finally adopted was a return to sym-metry, in so far as the east block became two equal rows of five cubes with the fourth back cube raised back an extra six metres; at this line, the eastern block was connected by a row of four cubes lengthwise at first floor level to the western block three cubic modules deep, from which the centre cube had been removed, next to a ramp leading up to the second floor at the end of the Temporary Exhibitions Gallery. Two additional cubes in front swung around to the left at the corner of the block and were joined to it by a bridge.

The eastern pair of five cubes were kept a quarter-module apart and this gap was extended the depth of the building. The public entrance of the museum ran back like a wide saw cut, forming a transparent channel between the two rows of cubes. It went straight from front to back; the intention was that this gap would be transparent, thus allowing people to see through the building from one side to the other.

Earlier, the main stair leading up to the second floor was positioned some way in on the side next to the Temporary Exhibitions Gallery; from there it led up to a mezzanine level before continuing on up to the longitudinal bridge. This proposed asymmetrical vertical circulation, however, was abandoned in favour of a main stair located in between the paired rows of cubes. This had the advantage of freeing them for other uses and situating them on the main staircase on the axis of symmetry.

There were similarities with other projects, either recently completed or in progress. Three branch bank buildings – the Ropponmatsu (1971), Saga (1972–73) and Nagasumi (1971) – for the Fukuoka Mutual Bank, all

21

20 Early perspective of Schematic Design IV-I-1 (December 1972) with the stepped roof above the temporary exhibition space; the building skin is covered by a uniform square grid which is carried through to the glass walls of the cubes. Note the staggered symmetrical staircase entry to the second floor level.

21 First floor gallery passage. The Temporary Exhibitions Gallery can be opened by means of double doors between the columns to expose the space to the park outside.

23

22

repeated the same device of a 1.2 metre universal grid of aluminium squares that was so repetitive, it was almost hallucinogenic. The most extreme application of the uniform grid surface was in the Saga Branch completed around the same time of the Gunma Museum's design. Gunma Museum was the logical culmination of this important experiment. The Kitakyushu City Museum of Art, which was designed after Gunma, repeated many of its themes – in particular, the two parallel tubular forms separated by a gap – but at Kitakyushu, the cubic tunnels straddled the museum base in a quite spectacular way. The angled alignment of the Kitakyushu temporary exhibition room near the entrance also repeated the composition of the Japanese Exhibition wing at Gunma. Indeed Kitakyushu can be seen as a kind of distillation of Gunma; the paired cubes of the entrance hall were enlarged and elevated so that the space exploded vertically between the paired muzzles of its huge double cannons aimed over the hilltop towards the city below.

The Museum of Modern Art, Gunma can be seen as the product of Isozaki's feeling that what he had achieved at the Festival Plaza at Expo 70 represented the end of Modernism. Having spent five intense years devising and supervising this bit of 'technological Dadaism', as Kenneth Frampton described the ambitious computerized mixed-media mass entertainment robot,[20] what resulted from it was something so empty in its pointless celebration of technology for its own sake, that it lacked any genuine content or significance. In his work at the Expo, Isozaki had outstripped Archigram and exceeded their wildest dreams, as expressed by their Monte

Carlo Entertainment Centre and Cedric Price's Fun Palace. Expo 70 offered little that was new beyond its seductive technocratic rhetoric and its overly optimistic promise of technology as an all-purpose utopian cure for humanity's ills.[21]

The leap into conceptual architecture For Isozaki, conceptual architecture presented itself as the logical next step. His subsequent infatuation with grid surfaces would appear to have been inspired by the Superstudio group (who began their activities in Florence in December 1966) and Sol Lewitt's minimalist sculptures,[22] but it was an avenue which increased rather than lessened the dematerialization of his forms. As a consequence, it moved in a direction sympathetic to Isozaki's earlier Milan 'Electric Labyrinth' (1968), to the extent that it reduced architecture to a 'momentary and experiential place'. The Palladium Club in New York (1983–85) later realized the same idea on a much grander scale.

Isozaki made it clear at the outset that it was his intention to avoid all historical references and connections with prior architectures. He has said in an interview:

'I was thinking much more conceptually [compared to Richard Meier's Bronx Developmental Center in New York]. I was thinking how to destroy the traditional sense of proportion and balance – those proportions based on the

24

25

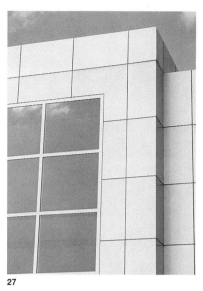

26

27

humanistic system of the Golden Mean from Greece, and the *kiwari* (the Japanese modular system) for wood structures. Le Corbusier developed proportions related to the Greek Golden Section and Kenzo Tange tried to combine the *kiwari* traditional Japanese proportions with the Fibonacci Series to make proportions like Le Corbusier.
'I wished to escape from these traditional systems of proportion. In the Oita Library, I tried to make the structural sections square and change the proportions from that to develop a facade based on a grid […] Adolfo Natalini tried to apply a grid mesh everywhere and was published in the late 1960s. It was at this time that I found the same idea expressed in Italy. It is exactly the same with the American Sol Lewitt. But the connection was not direct.
'The idea I started out with was to destroy the surface of the man-made element to render it homogeneous – yet without any significance or any meanings being involved. My aim was to negate any meanings arising from the surface. Any connection with Alvar Aalto and Gunnar Asplund were post-design.'[23]

In his questioning of the formal premises of architecture, Isozaki placed himself in the same relative position with regard to the role of the object in conventional art as American conceptual artists had done in the late 1960s. They sought to do away with the object and reduce it to a simple dematerialized geometric entity. Herein lies the significance of the universal grid – its purpose was to enhance the dematerialization of form and deny the corporeal nature of the artefact. Dematerialization became a major concern of conceptual artists in

the late 1960s, equalled only in importance by the emphasis on process; what it amounted to was the intention to make architecture as insubstantial, invisible and lacking weight, as the mental concepts from which the forms sprang. Thus it was almost literally an architecture which based itself on universal structures from the reasoning mind.

Conceptual art is generally conceded as having started with Marcel Duchamp whose work strongly influenced Isozaki. It was against this backdrop, and the elaboration of 1960s conceptual art, that Isozaki's dematerialization of the Gunma Museum and the pronounced neoplatonism manifested in his choice of cubes for its conceptual framework (not ignoring his trial experiments which set the scene) should be viewed.

When Sol Lewitt buried a steel cube in the earth at Bergeyk in The Netherlands in July 1968, his documentation of its visual disappearance in photographs paralleled Isozaki's decision to line the outside of his concrete cubic framework with shiny treacherous surfaces realized by the medium of reflective aluminium plates. Indeed, the diagrams which Isozaki made for Gunma are identical to Sol Lewitt's drawings for his sculptures. Not only did Isozaki beat Archigram in the techno-futurist stakes, he followed this up by producing what is arguably the first major international masterpiece of conceptual architecture.

The most intriguing aspect of this was that while Isozaki regarded the Festival Plaza as a dead end, it nonetheless served as the springboard for the next stage of conceptual architecture. The germs of the Festival Plaza lay

28

26 Corner of 12 m cube, entrance hall, the structure of columns and beams was hidden under a taut 2mm thick aluminium skin of identical square units joined along the centre line to suggest incompleteness.

27 Frame and glass infill of cubes shows the alternate patterning of joints and skin mullions.

28 Top southeast corner of the Japanese Gallery illustrates the wrap-around continuity of the aluminium sheath.

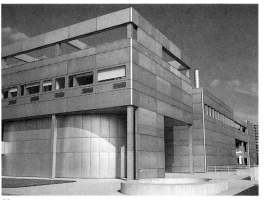

29

29 Bronx Developmental Center, New York, by Richard Meier, designed 1970–71, but not completed until 1976. The taut aluminium skin follows an orthodox Modernist streamlined aesthetic.

30 Conceptual sketch of the underlying cubic framework. Isozaki's design questions whether a cubical framework can act as a metaphor for the art museum.

31 South elevation. The solidity of the cube-frame lacks the transparency envisaged in the concept.

in the Milan Triennale 'Electric Labyrinth'. The Festival Plaza, in turn, did not imply architecture in any real sense as producing permanent structures; rather it relied on the presence of mobile 'apparatuses' which generated transient structures of movement, activities and 'atmospherics' more usual in theatre than in architecture.

It was the unbridled conceptual nature of the architecture which differentiated Isozaki's Gunma Museum from Richard Meier's streamlined Bronx Developmental Center, which, although it was designed in 1970–71, at approximately the same time as Isozaki's museum, was a much more orthodox Modernist work by comparison.[24] The preliminary sketches of the underlying cubic *parti*, together with the perspectives of the conceptual framework against a blank background or with the trees in the park showing through, reinforce this fact. They were diagrams of the concept, a concept which required the architecture to be, if not invisible, then visibly insubstantial and ethereal, something which in practice was impossible. Coincidentally, the conceptual approach intersected with Isozaki's initial impulse of including the green of the park in his architecture. In the sketches, the trees behind the museum were visible through the enlarged framework of cubes. This proved impossible to achieve because buildings are of necessity solid corporeal objects. A completely transparent art museum posed severe functional problems in terms of the display and preservation of works of art. The Gunma Museum avoided this contradiction by deploying highly reflective aluminium panels on the outside which, while they were not in any way transparent, provided the illusion of weightless non-existence.

This cubic conceptual framework was placed on a perfectly flat lawn to suggest the ideal conceptual domain of the museum in what was a very neoclassical gesture. At the same time, the frame doubled as the supporting skeleton for the building. In using both, the conceptual framework doubled as the structural frame. Isozaki later explained that the cube was his metaphor for the art museum.

The cube as metaphor and frame Isozaki was thus operating on two levels: using a basic structure comprised of the Gunma Museum's cubic framework to modulate the space additively giving rise to the primary form. At the same time, he deployed secondary ancillary or supplementary structures within the basic structure to create multiple layers in such things as sculptor Aiko Miyawaki's stepped *tokonoma*-like object at the far end of the entrance hall; the central marble stairway; the projected shadow lines from two cubes in the second floor auditorium; the large chair structures of the second floor offices, and the rotating screens of the side wall of the Temporary Exhibitions Gallery.

Art today is no longer tied to one place; rather, it is transported around the globe moving from one exhibition site to another. Once art is removed from its original context and placed inside a museum, and then migrates from museum to museum, it loses its connection with a specific time and place. Paintings and sculptures arrive in crates complete with their own frames and pedestals, and little else. The art museum might, then, be

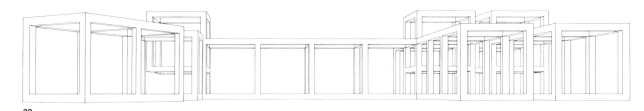

30

31

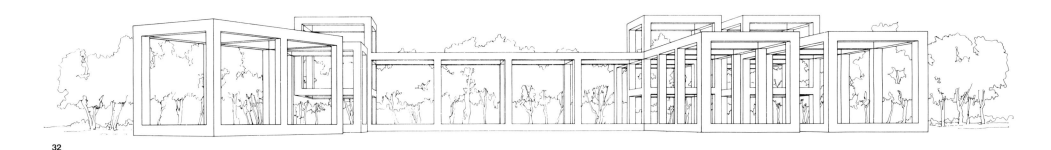

14   seen as little more than a large container and receptacle, for receiving, displaying and experiencing increasingly mobile works of art.

Isozaki decided that the Gunma Museum should operate largely as an enclosing framework with no explicit or associated iconography of its own.[25] He reasoned that, since its main function was to display works of art, the museum was a stage, and, as such, it needed the equivalent of a proscenium arch to frame the work of art in the same way that the proscenium arch frames the stage drama in theatre in the West or the stage of a Japanese Noh theatre. A cubic framework enclosing space in three dimensions therefore seemed a suitable metaphor for the art museum. But the spatial frame was far from being neutral iconography.

Frames do several things in Western art: they ensure a high degree of independence for what is inside them and they separate the art on display from what is around them; space is delimited by a border and its character is differentiated from that of its surroundings to indicate that it is a world of its own.[26] By isolating the work of art from its field, a new centre is created. The use of the frame as a metaphor for a museum devoted to modern art is highly suggestive in these terms. First, it detaches the museum from the landscape and limits it, proclaiming it to be a realm set aside from the everyday while labelling it a place specifically devoted to the art experience, at the same time that it designates it a man-made space. Within its confines, the art experience is intensified. It creates a new focus in order to direct attention to the art. In Japan the frame acts as a gesture which draws the

audience into its play of illusion and, conversely, it is a means of taking the inside into the landscape. Isozaki conceived his basic cubic framework as a neutral spatial entity for works of art, with the framework setting the works apart from the surroundings of the park. Yet it also draws the park ambiguously inside, while emphasizing that the act of viewing a work of art is a specialized aesthetic act in that it places the work in a new artificially delimited context.

Isozaki therefore magnified the frame in its role as a device for delimiting the space of a painting to the point that it included the museum. By extension, the museum can be seen as a cultural frame for art. Like the frame around a work of art, the museum alerts the visitor to the presence of art by eliminating anything that might distance the individual or lessen the intimacy of that experience.

In thinking about the nature of the art museum as distinct from the everyday, Isozaki created a three-dimensional structure which was foremost a representation of the museum in the second-half of the twentieth century. Accordingly, it was far from neutral, and more visible than Isozaki had originally intended. By pushing the formal rhetoric of neutrality so hard, Isozaki turned the Gunma Museum itself into an art object – the museum was transformed by the act of interrogating itself. Its neutrality was of the most assertive kind imaginable. Isozaki converted the museum into a large work of art that could stand by itself. Once this occurred it was no longer possible to maintain the fiction that the museum was neutral, much less invisible. As such, the Museum

32 The cubic framework isolates the work of art; at the same time it draws the park inside the museum so that the trees are seen behind it.

33 South entrance bridge, stage I, 1974, inserted in the gap between two rows of 12 m cubes.

34

35

of Modern Art, Gunma is one of the most formidable monuments to the modern art museum as a container for portable art in the twentieth century.

The floating museum The museum rests lightly on the green plane of lawn in Gunma-no-mori Park. The building was not tethered to the earth, and the square frame of each cube that goes across the bottom is identical to the side and top members. There was no distinction in terms of proportion between top, bottom and sides; there was no up or down, no narrowing of the square in recognition of the anisotropy of space to cope with the weight of the building mass. The aluminium-covered cubes appear to be weightless, floating as light as helium-filled balloons.

In choosing cubes and insisting that the reinforced concrete structure have the same dimensions throughout, and the beams and columns the same section (or nearly so), Isozaki ignored gravity.[27] Buildings are of course made from heavy materials such as concrete, steel and glass, and are therefore subject to a much greater extent than painting and sculpture to the pull of gravity. They respond to this external power by organizing their shapes around the vertical. Engineers have developed optimal sections, beams that are deeper than they are wide to resist bending moments, columns that are square or round to resist the different types of compression loads, and frames designed to make the most economic use of material.[28] The square and the cube belong to

an abstract neoplatonic system that is unconnected with the demands of gravity. Pure shapes like the cube thus imply a gravity-free environment such as outer space where materials have no weight.

The suggestion of weightlessness was strengthened by covering the surface of the building and hiding the structure of columns and beams under a taut skin of 2 mm thick aluminium panels composed of identical square units. This uniform square grid expressed unlimited extension in opposition to the cubic frame whose role was to delimit the museum. The visual extension of these forms was reinforced by avoiding edge joints at the corners. A close examination of the pattern of the aluminum panels revealed how the joints were positioned along the centre line of each vertical and horizontal top and bottom member that make up each large 12 m cube. The panels were bent around the corners to avoid a joint at the edge of each cube. Later, in 1994, when the museum was extended, a thicker 4 mm aluminium sheet was introduced which required joints at the corners. Although minor, this detail is significant because behind it lay the suggestion of incompleteness and a potential for extension by the addition of further cubes.

Squares balance the coordinates. Because the sides of a square are equal, no dimension is paramount and this produces an effect of stillness and repose rather than dynamic imbalance. The glazed walls of the large cubes were subdivided symmetrically into nine on each side so that each face is balanced in the horizontal and vertical directions around a central square panel. The sides were expressly divided to a basic rhythm of

15

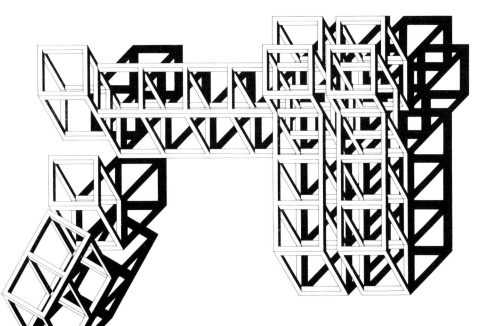

36

34 The Japanese Gallery is arbitrarily rotated 22½ degrees and stands in a large square pond.

35 The abstract human face supported on a pair of stubby legs of the southwest end of the Japanese Gallery wing advanced the dimension of Dadaism.

36 The skeletal structure of 12 m cubes evokes no distinct image and neutralizes the museum architecture.

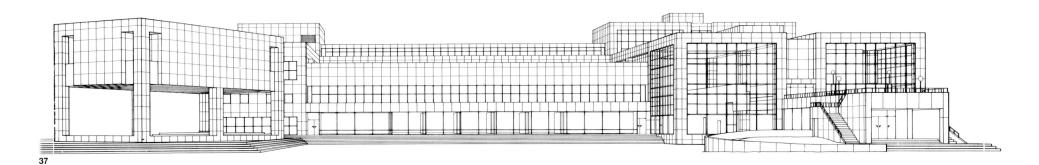

37

(a+a+a+a) a (a+a+a+a) – which alternatively can be read as A:A:a:A:A with each A unit equivalent to two 'a's. The 'a'-grid is interrupted at ground level by combining the small squares and dividing the width in four identical 'A'-sized square panels the same as two 'a's, thereby forming a door one by two 'a's high in the middle. Isozaki's aim was to make the cubes appear to float, and push the building skeleton into the background. The square format however created a number of practical problems because the beams could not be designed in an optimal way structurally with the depth they required to carry the loads. Isozaki recognized this: 'discrepancies and intersections of moderate degree are apparent in the entrance hall – a place in which the interior of the cube can be experienced in its true size [...] Pure abstract form and actual architecture follow different codes.'[29] Keeping the size of the posts and beams the same disrupted the flow of load from above to the beams and thence to the columns by dismissing the structural distinction between beams and columns, so their load-carrying function seems vague. The effect is one of lightness and upward rising freedom.

This had important ramifications because the soffits of the beams along the edge of each cube were exposed in the internal space of the Entry Hall and above the main stair, in places where they needed to appear the same in section even though the columns have very different structural jobs to do.

The dissolution of the corporeal artefact The source of Isozaki's denial of corporeality in the Museum of Modern Art is closely related to the crisis he suffered on completion of the Festival Plaza followed by his search for a new method. This gained a focus when he identified himself with the traditional Japanese motif of 'twilight gloom', in which shadows are banished and objects float freely in an undifferentiated enveloping fog,[30] resulting in a denial of corporeality. It entails reducing solid objects into abstract networks of lines and planes generated by an infinitely repeating grid of enormous symmetry. The museum is a mere fragment, an incomplete firming-in of a fraction of the universal 12 m grid which extended out indefinitely on the X, Y and Z axes. Contrast was avoided, in keeping with the mood of twilight, and colours were limited to off-white and pale grey. In the absence of strong light and shadows, the architectural forms appear as disembodied pieces of geometry. This further reinforced the image of the museum as a particularized fragment of universal space that reaches out to infinity.

The denial of corporeality involved a conception of the body as neither resisting nor transmitting forces, a body existing entirely outside the normal gravitational sphere in a weightless universe that is homogeneous and endless. And its effects can be observed in the relationship of the building frame to its skin. Structure is absorbed by the enclosing skin. Gunma's structure is debased, first, by ignoring the optimal sections for concrete beams and the convention of supporting and supported members, and secondly, by making the structural frame con-

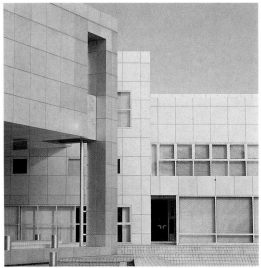

38

37 Perspective from the south. The surface is divided into equal square parts comprising standard aluminium panels and glass walls.

38 South elevation of the gallery at the Japanese Art wing hinge. The uniform abstract subdivision of the surface induces a sensation of weightlessness and dematerialization.

39

39 Positive and negative stepped squares beneath the Japanese Art wing introduced a hermaphroditic union of male/female.

40 Entrance stairs on either side of the access bridge along the central spine lead to the first floor.

41 The cubic south face of the entrance hall is subdivided into nine by nine squares, simplified at the bottom to A:A:a:A:A.

form to the square proportions of a cube. This debasement of the frame was taken one step further by hiding it under a uniform square grid of reflective aluminium panels. The grid was spun into an unbroken web over both the frame and its infill, without differentiating between wall and frame. The aluminium cladding fuses with the frame so it is impossible for the eye to follow the path of the forces down to the ground.

Isozaki deliberately split the surface in places so one can peek through the gaps and see the underlying skeleton. It is almost as though he were allowing the viewer to peer behind the stage scenery and flats at the stage machinery. Isozaki likens the effect to 'an occasional glimpse of the lining of someone's jacket. The skeleton is thus pushed into the background, leaving behind it a mere suggestion of its presence.'

Lightness of meaning On the outside, the Museum of Modern Art was stripped back so that little else remained besides the grid and a sleek mirror-like sheath of square aluminum panels. The erasure of anything which might add meaning was deliberate. Although the museum is intentionally neutral and its structure assimilated within the tense aluminium skin, it is not passive – rather, it urges us to question what is the nature of architecture by forcing architecture on this occasion to interrogate itself.

People tend to reject any absence of meaning – where there is nothing they often invent something in its place. The more empty and blank an object is, the more it draws in meaning from outside itself. The shimmering immateriality of Isozaki's museum, its general emptiness and the disturbing feeling of non-existence which emanates from it, challenges the individual to add something of his own. Isozaki explored the idea of an anti-expressionistic architecture which, unlike expressionistic architecture, throws our own image back at us. Ultimately we, as users and viewers, supply the message and imbue objects with significance. The Gunma Museum is an essay in the way that architecture acquires significance from the culture which created it.

The Japanese self-image is complicated. The English writer Peregrine Hodson alluded to the difficulties a Westerner experiences understanding Japan in describing how, when he neared the middle and approached the secret of Japan, '… one forgets where one is coming from, who one is and why one is there, so that by the time one actually reaches the centre of the maze and finds the secret of Japan, it has no meaning'.[31] If Japan is a mirage invented by the Japanese, then what is found in the maze is an illusion. In a strange way, the unreal quality of the Gunma Museum is a silent echo of the illusion that is Japan.

One way to avoid this is to recognize that Japan is a mental fiction – it is what the Japanese want it to mean. A blank, as exemplified by the Gunma Museum which reflects the images of those around it. Isozaki was intrigued by the way that architecture, in crossing the threshold of meaning, can acquire a new cultural significance. The Gunma Museum was a clever trap – a work which posed a question – to catch architecture.

The Museum of Modern Art, Gunma thus became a kind of imperfect mirror. The gaps and small cracks in the

40

41

42

42 First floor spine between the
two rows of cubes slices
through the museum form from
south to north.

43 Perspective from the south end
of the entrance hall illustrating
the reversed perspective of lines
converging on the viewer.

44 Carrara marble *tokonoma*
sculpture at the far end of the
entrance hall.

18   mirror permit us to glimpse fractures in the basic structure, imperfections such as the floor beams hidden by the balconies of the Japanese wing and the concrete behind the front paired cubes of the entry. The concrete roof beams of the entrance hall are a fraction narrower than the columns which support them. These discrepancies remind us that we do not see things distinctly but only through the lens of culture which distorts reality; they are ironic reminders to us of the mirror's existence. The tears in the fabric, then, expose the basic structure that lies beneath the tense stretched aluminium skin.

Nothing better symbolizes the mannerist idea of art than the mirror, with its inherent paradox, unreality, brilliance and magic.[32] These are the same qualities that Isozaki chose to emphasize at Gunma, for the museum, as Isozaki volunteered in his writings, has as much in common with mannerism as it has with conceptualism in art. Mannerism is obsessed with metaphor since it apprehends everything as being in a state of permanent change and interaction.[33] Goethe, for example, observed of poetry that there is a 'poetry without figures of speech that is itself one single figure of speech.'[34] The Gunma Museum is just such a single metaphor about the nature of culture and art – a metaphor writ large.

Isozaki has observed: 'A skeletal structure made up of abstract cubical frames is so conventional and comprehensible that on the contrary it evokes no distinct image. It is an effective way of neutralizing architecture, and if the surface is divided into equal, square parts, the architecture is further neutralized.' Although Isozaki does not venture to explain why it is necessary to wipe architecture clean, he does make it quite clear that it is his intention. In his museum Isozaki confronts us with a blank; by doing this, he makes it available to Japanese society and invites it to supply its own sets of meanings. With its imperfections, it allows us see what lies beyond this – the profound emptiness, the illusion, at the heart of every culture. The mirror contains no information of its own: what it has, what it says, is what we put there. In this sense, the Museum of Modern Art, Gunma is really a large experiment to see how architecture acquires meaning. The image in a mirror is only a virtual image.

Putting perspective in perspective At the far end of the museum entrance hall the space is terminated by a trick sculpture sheathed in polished Carrara marble. It rises in a series of steps to the first floor level. Inside the sculpture is an elevator. The vertical planes on the right converge towards the viewer. It is darker here and the marble gleams in a ghostly way in the available light. This is the principal, although by no means the sole ancillary object in the museum; however, it is undoubtedly the most prominent. The altar-like Carrara marble sculpture is situated on the left side past the main staircase as the visitor enters the museum; from here, it offers a powerful conclusion to this grandiloquent space. But it is a restless gesture that throws the space back on itself.

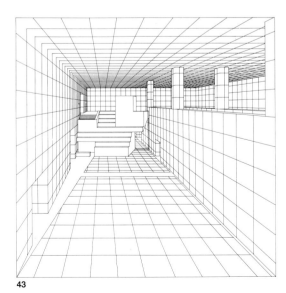

43

44

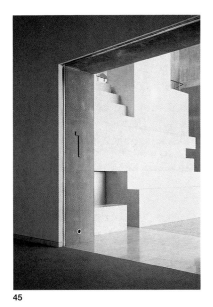

45

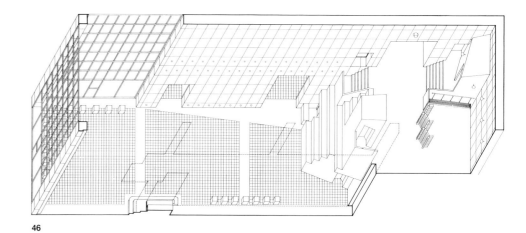

46

The four cube steps are too high to be climbed and the sculpture is more like a giant's staircase. A lift for the disabled is cleverly concealed inside it. The system of lines which radiate from the left side of the hall extends past the sculpture to the first floor. Here, six steps lead down from the main level to a balcony and a window overlooking the Temporary Exhibitions Gallery.

The sliced sides converge on the left-side wall in line with the start of the main staircase. The entrance hall's perspective is reversed at the back by the marble sculpture which flings its vanishing lines back into the eye of the viewer. Like a sling shot, it catches the vanishing movement before it is swallowed up, stops it, then catapults it back – the perspective of the hall is reversed and our visual expectations thrown into confusion.

The altar-object has other associations. Like the traditional picture recess or *tokonoma*, it is a strong statement about the spiritual and aesthetic significance of the museum. This part of the hall is reserved, as was the case with the *tokonoma* recess, solely for a piece of art to distinguish the spiritual importance of its location. The *tokonoma* recess was a rectangular frame as is this; it was accompanied by a decorative shelving recess, known as *tana* in Japanese. These are provided in the guise of the balcony which serves as enlarged *tana* shelves. Although the altar is Japanese, Isozaki's expression of it is Western. Isozaki deliberately encased it in Carrara marble, the material of Michelangelo and Italian Renaissance sculpture, to emphasize that perspective was a Renaissance invention. This is particulary fitting since Isozaki gained his international reputation as an architect by introducing the very latest in Western thinking to Japan, but he somehow manages to restate it in ways that are subtly, perhaps even unconsciously, Japanese.

In explaining the sculpture, Isozaki offered a Western art source, the painting *Giovanni Arnolfini and his Wife*, (1434), by Jan van Eyck.[35] This has a convex mirror mounted on the wall behind the couple which reflects the scene in front; but the mirror's field is larger than the artist's, resulting in a visual oxymoron, a picture within a picture in which the smaller miniature is not only greater in scope, but sees the scene in reverse. Instead of the room being terminated by a bare wall, it expands where it should disappear and this image is tossed back into the eye of the viewer, in much same way as occurs at Gunma.

Yet more curious illusions Nearly ten years before he designed the Gunma Museum, in 1963, Isozaki visited the Korakuen Magic House, a fun house with a maze of mirrors. He admitted afterwards, 'I can't help but recall the curious spatial experiences I had at the amusement park. They were indeed crazy'.[36] Isozaki was intrigued because he believed that the experiences in the Korakuen Magic House hinted at ways to create space with new qualities by the introduction of surprise traps, illusions and events. This was the source of a number of the spatial illusions in his museum and such things as the shadow traces of the two cubes projected onto the walls and ceiling of the auditorium.

47

45 Marble *tokonoma* stepped sculpture from the adjoining Temporary Exhibitions Gallery. Its faces converge towards the side wall in a manner calculated to reverse the hall perspective.

46 Axonometric of the entrance hall illustrates the reversal of perspective.

47 Jan van Eyck, *Giovanni Arnolfini and his Wife*, 1434. A convex mirror on the wall reverses the scene and disrupts the order of the pictorial space.

48

49

The auditorium is located on the first floor opposite the main stair. The main stair is enclosed on two sides by walls faced in reflecting marble in between which is an unpolished central strip of unreflective stone (since covered by a carpet runner) that is slightly narrower than the stair. The stair rises through the gap between two rows of 12 m cubes sandwiched between the entrance hall and administration that ploughs its way through the museum. The width of the stair is difficult to estimate because it is reflected in the polished marble walls on either side, giving the illusion that it extends infinitely.

At the point where the stair axis strikes the auditorium, Isozaki inserted a sliding door; above this is a glazed opening with louvres that operate electrically. On the auditorium wall opposite there is also a matching window and louvres. Thus, although fire-safety precautions made it impossible to continue the physical gap between the paired row of cubes the full depth of the museum from front to back, the axis of symmetry has been extended.

Inside the auditorium, the space is raised and lowered by cubic frames across it. Within these are two points, the first in line with the front line of seats, the other in the middle of the stage area, where small cubes were placed with lights inside them at their geometric centres. The first cube was tilted in an unstable manner, the second is parallel to the building grid so that when its shadow traces are projected on the wall, they form a series of concentric squares. The shadow lines of the twelve edges of the cubes were rendered on the off-white walls and ceilings as thin grey stripes. In some traditional Japanese restaurants the shadows of butterflies, in like manner, are presented as flickering images on the walls.

Underneath the Japanese Art wing, at the west end of the central Temporary Exhibitions Gallery, the floor is modelled by a pair of stepped concentric squares, one for each cube bay: one steps up, the other down; one is a positive convex form, the other is a mirror negative concave version. These interpret in an abstract way the traditional 'moon-viewing' platform, a game beloved by Renaissance architects; here, however, the tiled surface and grid is more reminiscent of the Italian Superstudio Group. Kenneth Frampton characterized it as a hermaphroditic union of male and female.[37]

These positive and negative stepped squares were covered by the new restaurant addition in 1994 (stage II of the design). This was a single-storey transparent pavilion with a terrace on its roof which continued the north–south geometry of the main central museum wing. It covered only part of the platform, the rest of which was used as an outdoor extension next to the reflecting pool.

Anatomy of the Museum of Modern Art After the Yom Kippur War between Israel and Egypt in October 1973, the Arab Nations limited oil production which precipitated a world energy crisis. The Japanese economy was severely affected. The 'oil shock' occurred one year into the construction of the museum, directly affecting its

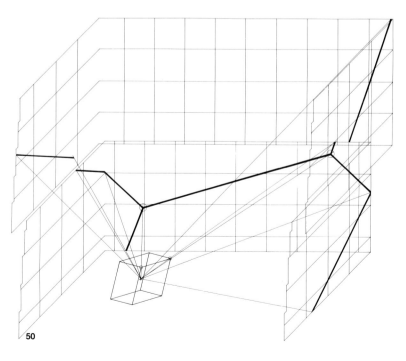

50

48 Polished marble staircase gives the illusion of indefinite extension.

49 Interior view of the Japanese Art Gallery.

50 Two cubes generating shadow traces on the walls of the first floor auditorium disrupt the cubic order.

51 Shadow lines on the wall of the auditorium.

51

52

52 Understorey of Japanese Gallery from the south pond before the stage II addition of a restaurant.
53 View from inside the new restaurant towards the pond.
54 West view of Japanese Art wing before the restaurant was added.

completion. Two things were involved: building materials, such things as window sashes, glass and carpet, suddenly became unobtainable and inflation rose fifty per cent in eighteen months. This caused many problems on the site which were further exacerbated since the Japanese bureaucracy was slow in dealing with them. Some materials were therefore changed and the Prefectural Government was forced to find additional funds to cope with the emergency. In the end, the west wing for traditional Japanese art was donated by the stockbroking company Yamatani Co.

The final museum scheme was settled in mid-February 1972 with the emergence of Schematic Design IV-2-1. With it the essential form was established but minor changes continued to be made. The plan consisted of three parts: a central steel-framed temporary exhibitions room with storage behind it, above which was a gallery for permanent exhibitions, the entire thing 36 m deep; and two bookends. The main entrance and public reception was at the east end farthest from the park entrance; this was complemented by a two-cube west wing containing vertical circulation and a ramp, tea ceremony space, at the corner of which was hinged a first floor gallery containing a permanent exhibition of traditional Japanese art. This stood on six *pilotis* and the space below it was used for sculpture. The Temporary Exhibitions Gallery is lower than the rest of the museum, being 48 m long, 18.6 m deep, and only 7.2 m high inside. It has an area of approximately 890 m² and is stepped from front to back to lift it to the same height as the east wing in line with the Permanent Exhibitions Gallery. The east wing has a

1.8 m clerestory above the main stair with the reinforced concrete structure 2.4 m higher than the wing.

The entrance, though less elaborate than the Kitakyushu City Museum of Art, is much the same in principle. It was inserted in the gap between two strong transverse square forms on the cross axis. Kitakyushu sits on a steep hill, resulting in an entrance that is a much more monumental affair than Gunma's which is on a flat site. In plan, however, they look very similar. A long bridge extends out from the front of the Gunma Museum ending in a nub of two identical staircases with a semicircular ramp on the left side. The visitor can enter the museum directly or mount the stairs and enter at first floor level to reach the coffee shop and the auditorium. From this upper level the visitor overlooks the main stair and the entrance hall on the left. The entrance hall is three bays deep (36 x 12 x 10.8 m high) giving it a proportion of roughly 30:10:9. Opposite it are located administration, the office of the Director, a conference room, and large machine room at the back. The goods entrance and loading bay sit directly across the axis of the main stair. This is convenient for access to storage rooms for Western paintings, crafts and sculpture and Japanese painting, and the large display furnishings storage.

The Temporary Exhibitions Gallery has 18 hanging rails 14.6 m long which can be raised and lowered electrically for hanging exhibition panels. In between the columns on the south wall, doors can be closed to isolate the exhibition or left open as desired to extend the space and include the gallery beside it which provides a public connection leading from the entrance hall to the tea ceremony room in the west wing behind the ramp.

53

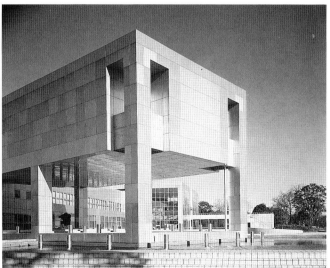

54

55 The new stage II restaurant, inserted beneath Japanese Art wing.

56 A freestanding platform on four columns within the east cube was used as a first floor coffee shop.

57 Interval between the coffee shop secondary structure and the larger cube-frame.

55

22 The first floor has a staff room, library, atelier, with the auditorium at the back. In the Schematic Design IV-2-1 the Permanent Exhibitions Gallery's nib walls were proposed between each bay, but these were subsequently omitted. A low 3.3 m high dropped central panel hides the overhead skylight and runs the entire length of the gallery space for the full five bays or 60 m. This admits reflected indirect daylight into the gallery. Providing natural light in art galleries has long been a concern of Isozaki and the skylight with its suspended reflecting surface represents a simplification of previous ideas for Gunma.

A bridge beside the ramp at the end of the first floor Permanent Exhibitions Gallery leads to the Japanese Art Gallery which is fully enclosed except for the corner balconies behind the columns. The lighting is subdued here and the atmosphere is one of luxurious reticence. The space possesses an unexpected warmth and classical repose following the powerful tectonic displays of the entry wing. The museum plan is basically an open 'U' with no connection at first floor level across the front south elevation. The circulation is driven between additive cubic units defined by column points and formal axes rather than natural movement systems; this results in interiors that leap from cube to cube.

The cube surfaces were kept as transparent as possible by employing narrow 96 x 660 mm deep cut-Ts to ensure the window divisions were slender. In the 1994 addition these were built up from welded plates. The result is a notable tour de force in the glass corners of the entrance hall which produces stunning vistas, especially along the terrace leading to the Japanese Art wing and the park. Each window is divided into thirty-six square frames that read either as distinct images on their own, or fuse in an overall image framed by each cube.

The interior swirls up and around the freestanding structure of the coffee shop inside the right cube that becomes a room within a larger room especially when viewed from outside. But the most dynamic and powerful effect is reserved for the main stair which charges up onto the first level, seeming to expand sideways by the reflections in the polished marble surfaces, then divides into two streams around the semi-cylindrical landing of the machine room stair standing in the way at the top and blocking the transverse axis.

Breaking symmetry: stage II in 1994 The Gunma Museum is not symmetrical, but it looks as though it should be. It is incomplete as it stands. From left to right it consists of four parts, two of which are identical A, B, C : C. To complete the bilateral symmetry all that is needed is to add two more parts, A, B, C : C, and (B, A) to it. Mentally, we are prompted to supply the mirror or flip image.[38] The presence of 'C' – an identical row of cubes on the right side, balancing the left side of the symmetry axis (which Isozaki stressed by locating the main stair on it) – strengthens the presumption of bilateral symmetry.

In not responding to the expectation of bilateral symmetry of the original museum composition in the 1994

56

57

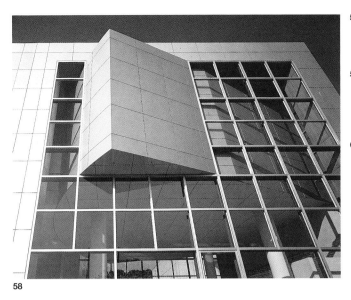

58

58 The semicircular shaped theatre pushes through the glass wall of the new extension completed in 1994.

59 The first floor Highvision Theatre side voids vaguely recall Isozaki's Oita Medical Conference Hall of over twenty years earlier.

60 The minimal steel stair with tempered glass balustrade leads to the first floor foyer between the browsing room and the Highvision Theatre; view from the entrance hall.

stage II addition, Isozaki violated its implied bilateral symmetry and this induces an air of instability. Symmetry signifies well-proportioned, well-balanced, and it denotes a concordance of the several parts. Beauty is usually associated with symmetry and the appreciation of pattern. This was ignored with the addition of a cube to the main entrance facade. The flip image of the identity (A, B, C) thus has no counterpart. This addition of the High-vision Theatre in a single cube represented only a minor departure but it cannot possibly counterbalance the weight of the identity. The result is a visual conundrum.

Instead of completing the bilateral symmetry Isozaki broke it. There were strictly practical reasons for this – the most obvious was the proximity of Masato Otaka's 1979 Gunma Prefectural Museum of History 15 m away from the Museum of Modern Art which prevented further expansion in this direction. The new stage II addition is small, no more than a single 12 m cube, plus the restaurant which occupies part of the open area beneath the existing Japanese wing.

A third stage is planned which envisages three exhibition rooms behind the first floor Permanent Exhibitions Gallery to increase the exhibition area of the museum by 1152 m² (equivalent to eight 12 x 12 m bays). Beneath the north extension there would be storage areas and a large machine room, an elevator and stair. The three new A, B, and C exhibition rooms would be linked directly to the Permanent Exhibitions Gallery by corridors at either end. The outer bay directly under the new exhibition rooms would stand on *pilotis* so

vehicles can reach the loading bay. None of this would be visible from the south on the park side of the museum.

In the 1994 addition, the axis in the front right cube is rotated in an east–west direction by the new addition; this is underlined by pulling back the first floor to leave a void on either side of the Highvision Theatre in a manner that vaguely recalls Isozaki's Oita Medical Conference Hall (1970–72). Much movement is generated between the ground and first floors. A minimal steel stair with tempered glass balustrade leads up to the foyer in between a browsing room and Highvision booth, and the Theatre itself. This first floor is relatively uncluttered and spartan with its white tiled floor. The information counter is under the new stair in the reception hall; beyond this is the museum shop on the north side adjacent to the passage leading to the History Museum.

The modest 140 sq m Theatre seats 42. It has a fan shaped plan with a slide projection room at the back and projection room at the front for illustrated lectures. The back, through which people enter, is circular and this protrudes through the cube to the outside producing an interpenetration of the two volumes: the smaller solid wedge of the Theatre, encased by the larger volume of the sturdy silver aluminium frame of the single 12 m cube, breaks through on the outside. The radial sides of the Highvision Theatre are interrupted where they strike the glass face of the cube by a wedge cut to accommodate the mullions. Inside, the space rebounds up and down in the voids between the walls and the first floor.

59

60

61

61 The fan-shaped Highvision
Theatre seats 42.

62 The outdoor eating terrace in
front of the new restaurant.

63 Aiko Miyawaki's kinetic *utsurohi*
sculpture. The flexible steel rods
springing from the pond move
continually in the breeze.

24   The new restaurant replaced the original 50 m² second floor coffee shop above the entry which was converted into the browsing room in the 1994 addition. The stepped square floor of the sculpture display area under the Japanese Art Gallery was levelled and the restaurant pavilion extended out from the existing part at right angles. It is three times larger (152.8 sq m) and has a separate kitchen. The great gain was a covered outdoor eating area under the *pilotis* surrounded by the pool with its *utsurohi* steel sculpture and outlook to the park. To take advantage of the park prospect, Isozaki designed a minimal pavilion with glass walls on three sides and generous sliding doors which open onto the *pilotis*-terrace. A circular stair by itself on the centre line of the restaurant between the mid-columns provides access to the restaurant roof. The rectangle of the restaurant is aligned with the larger rectangle of the pool, so that the plan becomes a montage of three patterns; the Japanese art wing at 22½ degrees overlays the pool which in turn is overlaid by the smaller rectangle of the restaurant.

The trees surrounding the Japanese Art wing frame the space around it and form a wall of dark foliage that contrasts with the waving silver wands of Aiko Miyawaki's steel sculpture which spring from the pool like graceful ballet dancers. These flexible bent rods, fixed to circular plates on the pool-bed, sway gently in the breeze, their delicate trembling movements matching the ripple patterns of the water. Like finely drawn reeds, the steel rods form three-dimensional networks of lines, incised into the scenery that surrounds the museum.

Mathematically, a uniform, featureless plane such as the lawn in front of the Gunma Museum has a vast amount of symmetry,[30] like a wall painted a single colour or Isozaki's mood of 'twilight gloom'. The same can be said for the infinite extension of a grid. The Museum of Modern Art, Gunma, is a calculated example of symmetry breaking; it illustrates something that happens in nature when symmetry gets lost and is replaced by pattern; and this is a paradoxical phenomenon. The Gunma Museum's pattern of 12 m cubes is a minor incident in a much larger 12 m grid that extends outwards indefinitely. If Isozaki's architecture, at this point, appears quirky and contrary, it is because he plays the game of symmetry breaking by building an architectural pattern that leads to bilateral symmetry, and then breaks it.

At the close of day, rows of tiny lights on the two walls of the entrance hall ride out into the landscape beyond like lines of tracer fire or the lights of an airport runway in front of the cockpit-window of a landing jet aircraft. As brightness falls and evening gathers in the twilight, the entrance hall advances and night presses up against the glass outside the museum. From the first floor, the lights dwindle to ever-finer pin pricks as they rush forward into indefinite blackness. The cube of luminescence, till now contained, safe and demarcated, joins the enveloping darkness. By interrogating art, architecture becomes more like a work of art. Isozaki's Museum of Modern Art, Gunma, is absorbed into the featureless plain of night, its broken symmetry now part of a far greater, infinite symmetry.

62

63

Above View showing the
Japanese Gallery from the west.
Right Japanese Gallery from
the southwest, showing the end
of the elevated *pilotis*-supported
gallery, and the new glass and
steel restaurant and terrace
below.

Left Detail looking east, showing the bridge upper connection between the Temporary Exhibitions Gallery and Japanese Gallery rotated at 22½ degrees to align with the park entrance.
Below View looking west, with the low gallery and tiled terrace framing the flat lawn, and the tilted Japanese Art wing beside the central entry spine.

Left The west cube beside the central stair and entry spine serves as a frame around the entrance hall.

Above East extension from the southeast; the volume of the fan-shaped Highvision Theatre projects through the glazed face of the newly added cubic frame.

Right The entry bridge and circular ramp lead to the first floor spine access between two rows of cube-blocks. This interspace between the two rows is expressed as a gap within the building itself.

Above The Highvision Theatre
breaks through the facade.
Right View along the first floor
access bridge with the newly-
designed 'stage II' cube and
Highvision Theatre interrupting
the earlier symmetry.

Left Entrance hall, view looking southeast: the transparency of the walls leads the space into the park.

Above View looking west from the entrance hall across the gallery to the Japanese Art wing. The external perspective is reduced to an abstraction by the overlay of the uniform square grid of window mullions.

Right Carrara marble-faced stepped sculpture by Aiko Miyawaki at the end of the entrance hall deliberately reverses the natural perspective and throws the space back on itself.

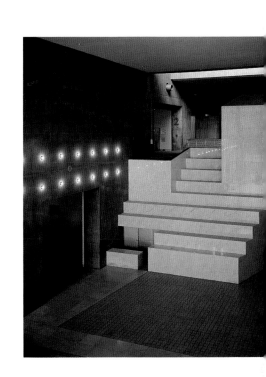

Left Main stair: the calculated dissolution of the physicality of the staircase, which is mirrored on the polished wall, gives the illusion of indefinite lateral extension.

Below The stair beside the waiting area (outside the auditorium on the first floor) extends the false perspective of the entrance hall.

Right The 36 m deep central steel-framed Temporary Exhibitions Gallery, with the circulation ramp at the end. The suspended 14.6 m long rails below the ceiling can be lowered electrically for hanging exhibition panels.

Below right First floor gallery passage with the doors to the Temporary Exhibitions Gallery closed.

Above and right Permanent Exhibition Gallery. Daylight is admitted by means of a central skylight shielded by a lower suspended horizontal ceiling panel.

Above Auditorium, view towards the front. Shadow lines from the cube are painted on the side wall and ceiling.
Right Auditorium, view of the rear wall.

Below left The new Highvision Theatre seats 42, with a slide projection room at the back and a projection room at the front for illustrated lectures.
Below right Side entrance to the Highvision Theatre.

Above Browsing room in the new extension, with the Highvision Theatre behind.
Left View across the browsing room.
Right View looking east; the new steel and glass staircase leads from the foyer to the Highvision Theatre.

Left Freestanding first floor
structure within the east
entrance cube, with the new stair
connection.
Right Ground floor connection
to Masato Otaka's adjoining
Gunma Museum of History. An
information counter is under the
new stair, beyond on the left lies
the museum shop adjacent to
the passage leading to the
Museum of History.

Left A minimal steel spiral stair connects the outdoor dining terrace to the roof of the new glass-enclosed restaurant pavilion beneath the existing Japanese Art wing.
Right View looking south across the dining terrace to the pond.
Below Pond and Aiko Miyawaki's *utsurohi* sculpture in the water.

Above left Al fresco dining terrace under the Japanese Art wing, at its southwest corner. **Above right** View from the edge of the pond.

Site plan

1 main entrance
2 car park
3 Gunma-no-mori Park
4 museum entrance
5 Museum of Modern Art,
   Gunma
6 History Museum
7 Highvision Theatre and
   museum shop
8 restaurant
9 storage
10 contemporary exhibition
   room
11 pond
12 service road

Drawings

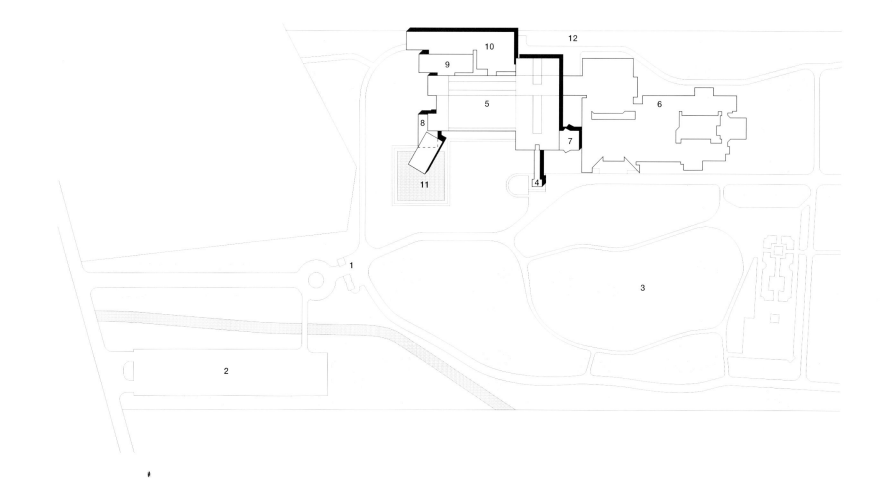

0   50m

0   150ft

Ground floor plan

1 main entrance
2 entrance hall
3 reception
4 Temporary Exhibitions
  Gallery
5 gallery
6 hall
7 outdoor sculpture area
8 pond
9 stairs to terrace
10 restaurant
11 kitchen
12 Browsing Room
13 *Cha-shitsu* tea ceremony
  room
14 ramp
15 museum shop
16 goods entrance
17 loading bay
18 storage: Western paintings
19 storage: crafts and sculpture
20 storage: Japanese paintings
21 storage: display furnishings
22 storage
23 wcs
24 staff entrance
25 director's office
26 office
27 staff wcs
28 plant

50

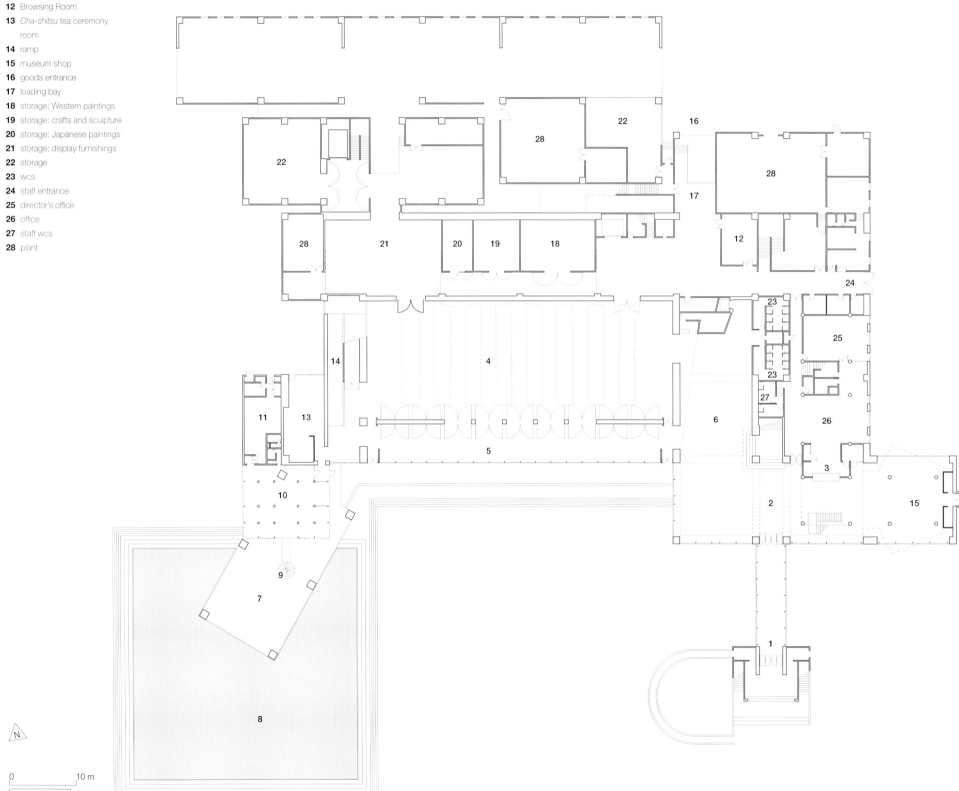

0   10 m

0   30ft

First floor plan

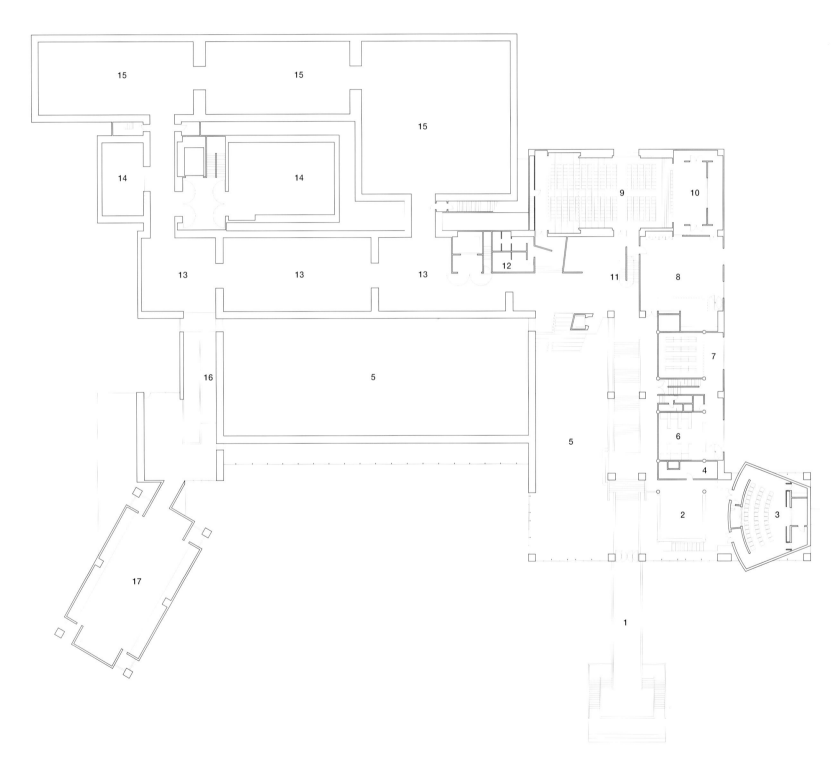

51

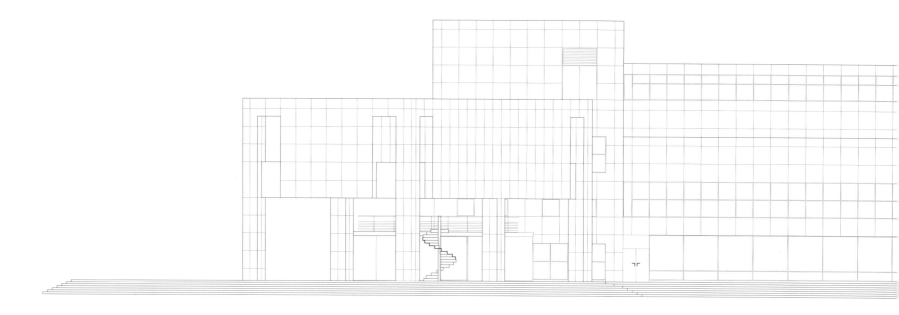

South elevation

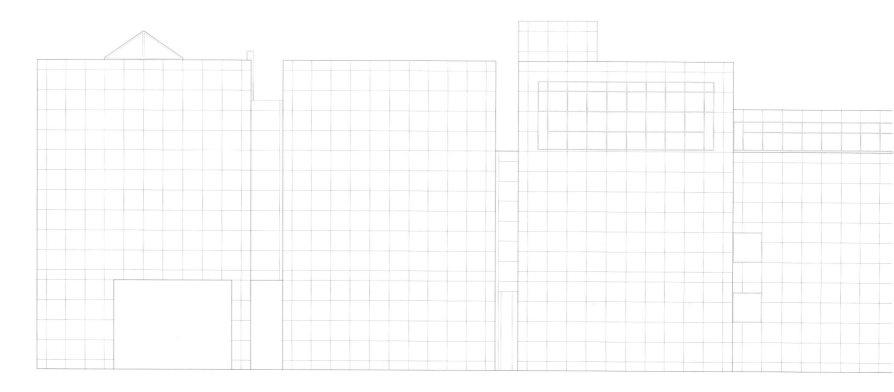

West elevation

52

0   5 m

0   15ft

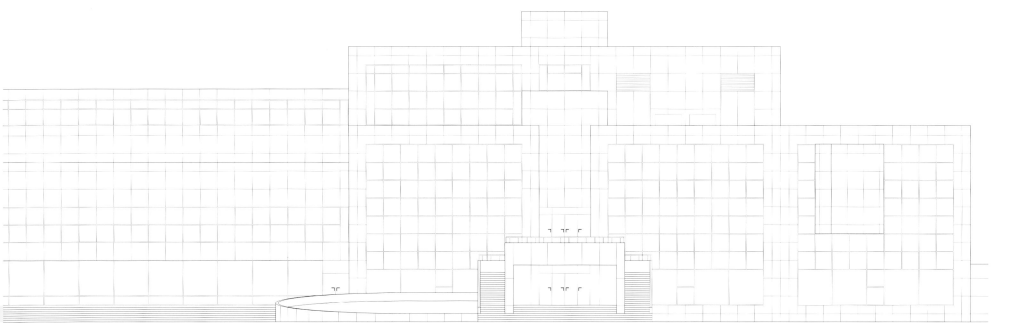

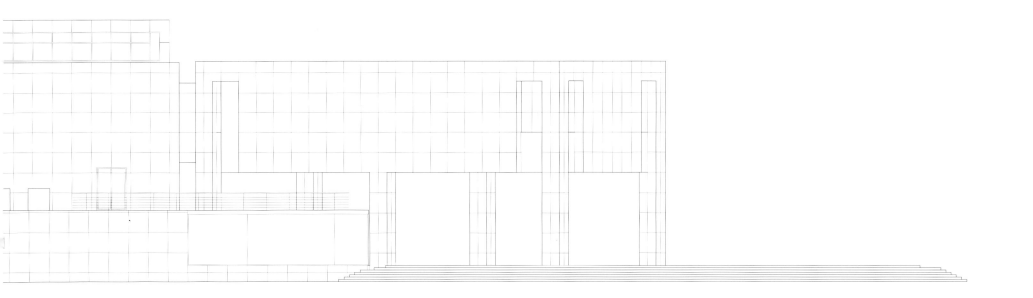

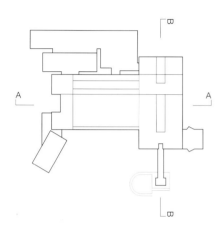

54

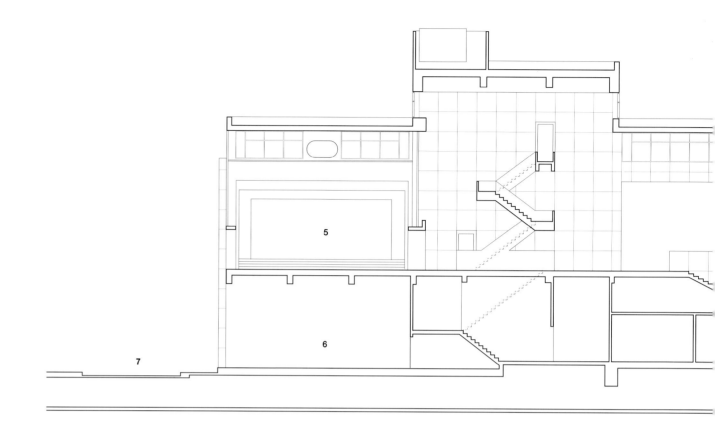

Section B

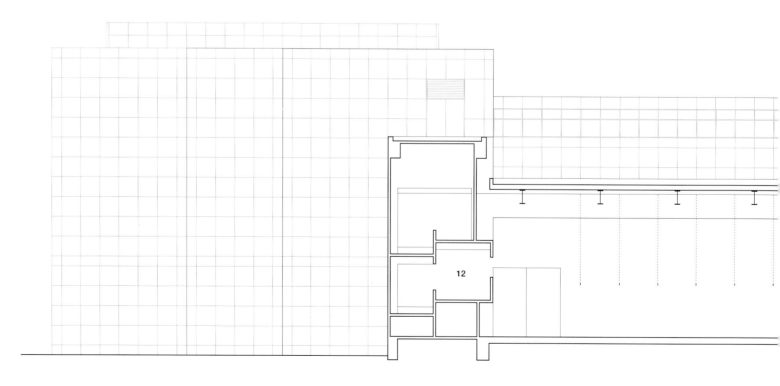

Section A

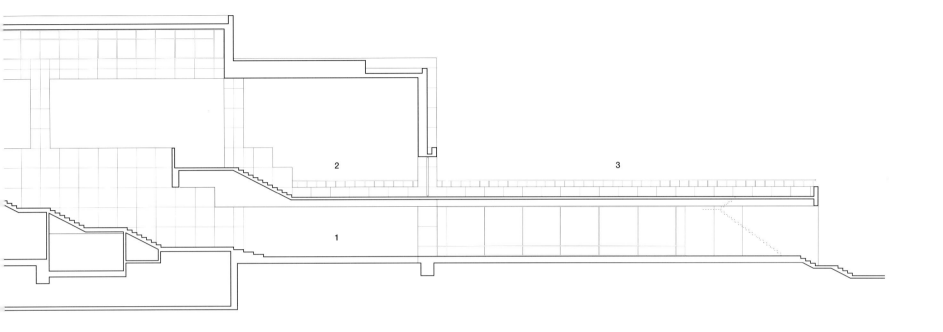

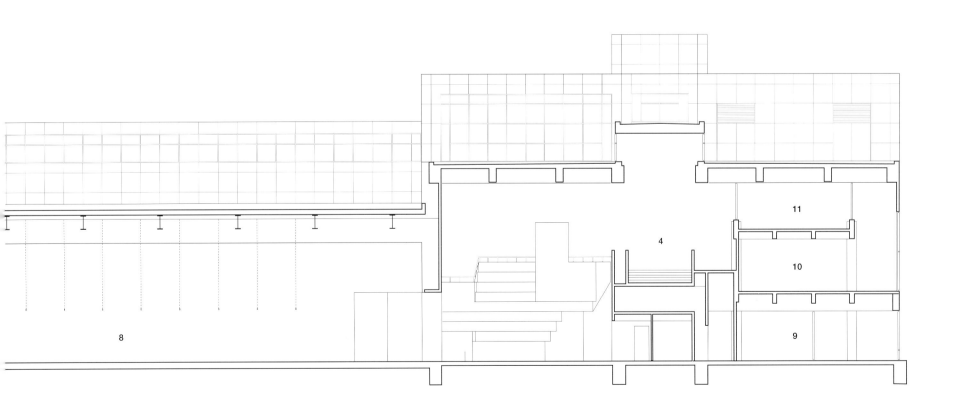

Section through Permanent
Exhibitions Gallery
1 skylight
2 Permanent Exhibitions
Gallery
3 art storage

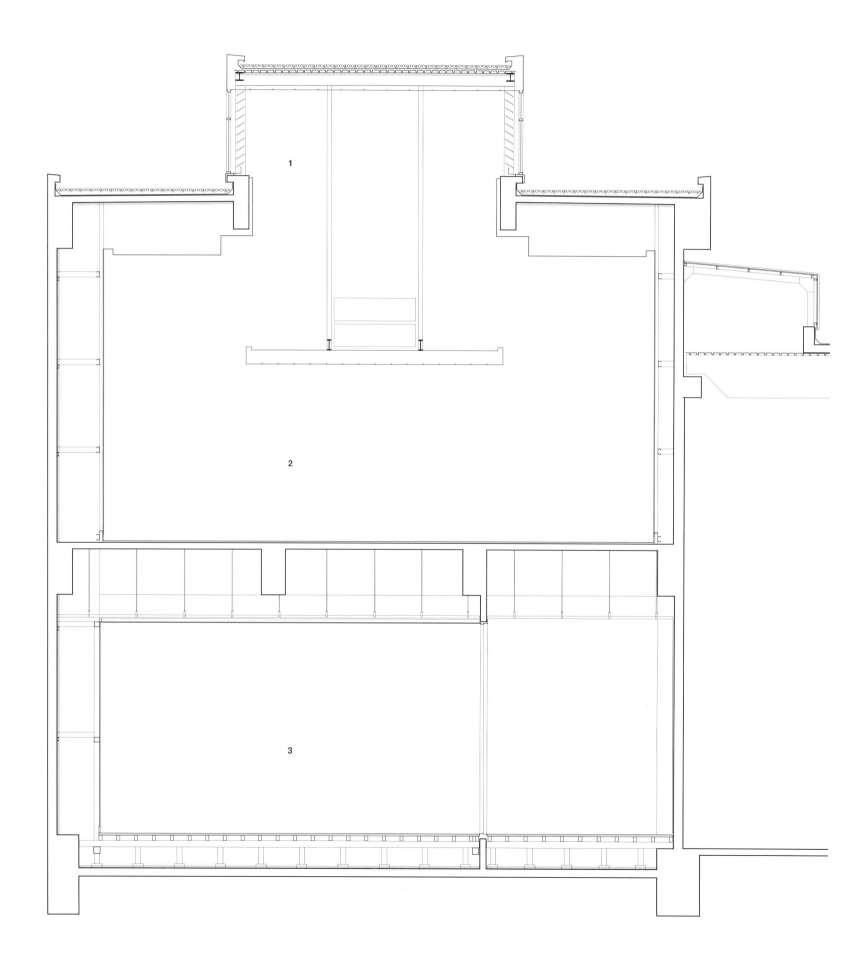

0   1m

0   3ft

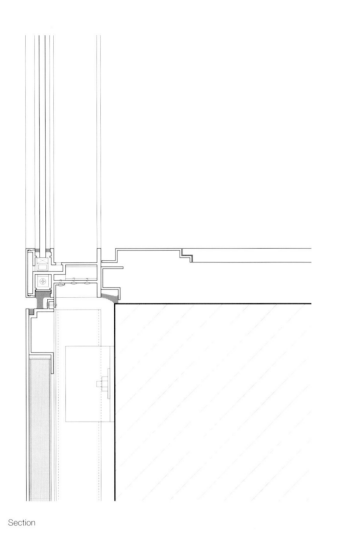

Section

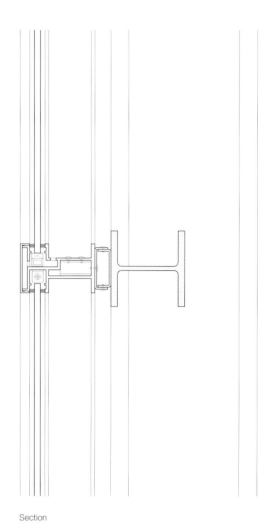

Section

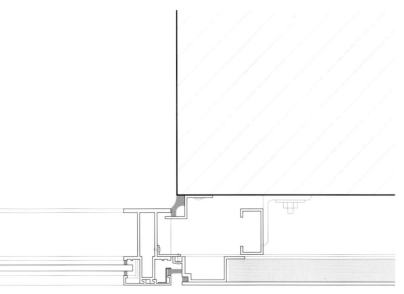

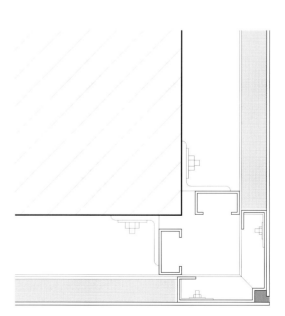

0   100mm

0   4in

Plan

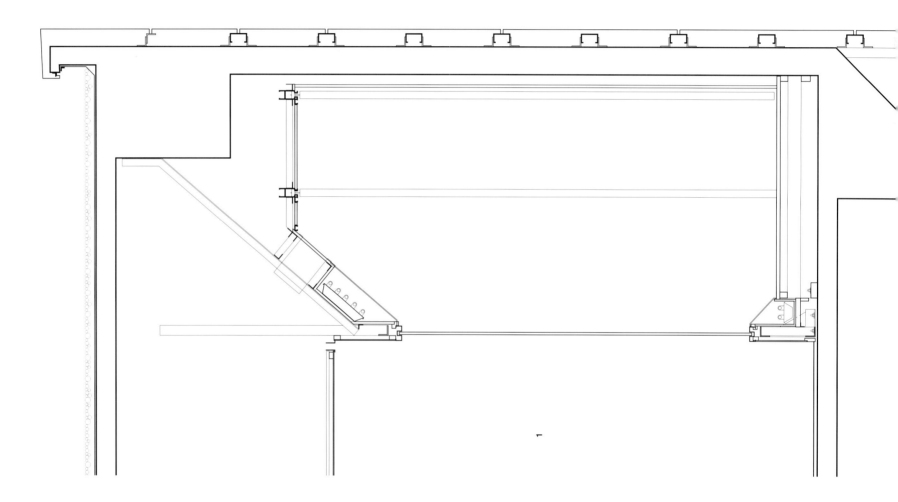

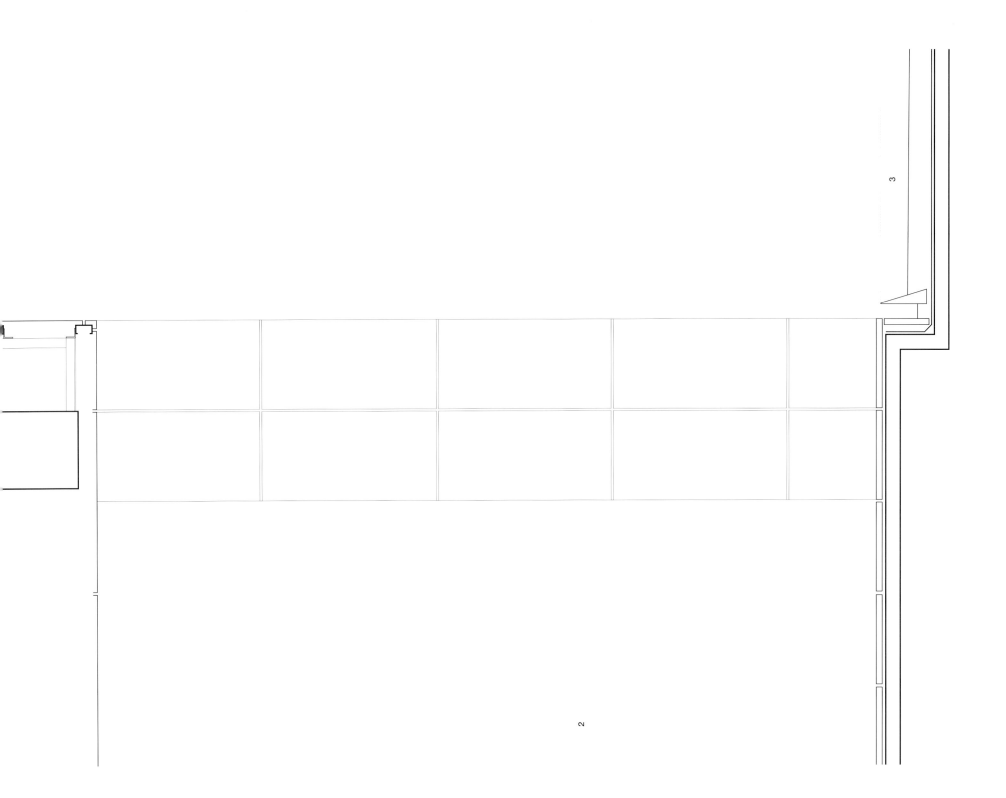

Photographic acknowledgements

Photographs for the essay section courtesy of Arata Isozaki & Associates and Yasuhiro Ishimoto. Additional photographs supplied by Philip Drew: figs 3, 29; *Japan Architect*: fig 25; Osamu Murai: fig 49; Yoshio Takase: figs 3, 5.

Notes

1 See 'Personal Notes on the Cube', *Japan Architect*, Vol 51, No 3 (March 1976), pp 24–26, in which Isozaki records the use of the cube in his work.

2 Bruno Taut, *Houses and People of Japan*, 2nd ed, (Tokyo: Sanseido,1958), p 3.

3 *Ibid*, p 53.

4 See *Gunma Profile* (Japan: Gunma Prefecture), with Preface by Ichiro Shimizu. Gunma means 'place of horses'. The prefecture has an area of 6,356 sq km (2,453 sq m) and the total population of the prefecture in April 1985 was 1.97 million. It is described in *Japan: An Illustrated Encyclopedia*, Vol 1, p 480, as, '…long a centre of raw silk and cereal production, Gunma has recently shifted to vegetable farming to supply the Tokyo market.'

5 William Horsly and Roger Buckley, *Nippon New Superpower: Japan since 1945* (London: BBC Books, 1990), pp 172–3.

6 Bruno Taut, *op cit*, p 305, wrote: 'So we went back to Takasaki, to our little house in Shorinzan and enjoyed for the last time the beauty of the country.' From his farmhouse, Taut could glimpse the bold outline of the Haruna range.

7 Arata Isozaki referred to Bruno Taut's contribution in his Foreword to *Botond Bognar, Contemporary Japanese Architecture: Its Development and Challenge* (New York: Van Nostrand Reinhold, 1985), p 10. Bognar credited Taut with reviving interest in the Japanese in the architecture of *shoin*, p 51, but criticized his biased modernist view of Katsura which ignored its brilliant, gorgeous, sometimes gaudy elements, p 82.

8 See *Arata Isozaki 1959–1978, GA Architect*, No 6 (Tokyo: ADA Edita, 1991), p 116.

9 See Bognar, *op cit*, p 143.

10 *Arata Isozaki, op cit*, p 116.

11 The first scheme that resembled the final museum design Schematic Design IV–1–1 was dated 21 January 1972. This comprised two parallel rows of five cubes separated by a narrow gap, the fourth from the front was elevated above the rest, and the long stepped gallery was terminated by two cubes at its western end with each cube separate. In front, a hinged pair of cubes was rotated to face the park entrance. The composition was symmetrical.

12 Listed as No 7, Gunma-no-mori Schematic Design I, No 710430 (dated 30 March 1971).

13 See Gunma-No-Mori Schematic Design I, 710430.

14 Document: Schematic Design II, No 710630 (dated 30 June 1971).

15 See Gunma Museum Schematic Design I–1, A Type 710605 (5 June 1971).

16 I refer to each Schematic Design series by number because Isozaki produced some twenty-eight documents in four series between April 1971 and April 1972. The important series are GM No 6 Schematic Design I–1: A. B.C.D. Type (5 June 1971) and GM No 10, Schematic Design I–2: A.B.C.D. Type (23 July 1971). In the second series each type is developed further.

17 Schematic Design I–1, 710605.

18 Schematic Design I–2: Type-D, 710723.

19 Schematic Design II–1, 711004 (4 October 1971)

20 See Kenneth Frampton, 'Post-Metabolism and the Dissolution of Architecture: Amplification and Neutrality 1960–75', in *Arata Isozaki, op cit*, p 105.

21 See Arata Isozaki, 'Festival Plaza, Expo '70, Osaka', in *Arata Isozaki, op cit*, p 86. He writes: 'I dropped out emotionally and the exposition seemed to me less like a huge festival and more like a meaningless ruin. It was to disappear in six months…'

22 Isozaki's conceptual drawings and sketches for the Gunma Art Museum of Art closely parallel Sol Lewitt's schematic diagrams and generational form series for his sculptures. For a comparison, see *Sol Lewitt Structures 1962–1993* (Oxford: Museum of Modern Art, 1993), *Drawing for Seven Structures*, Plate 65; *Cube Base*, Plate 53; and *123* (1978) Plate 66.

23 In an interview with the author at his Aksa house at Karuizawa, Nagano Prefecture on 21 September 1994. In *The Making of a Modern Japanese Architecture: 1868 to the Present* (Tokyo: Kodansha International, 1987), pp 255–56, David B Stewart states that parts of Gunma Museum evoke such works as the Viipuri Library by Aalto and the Stockholm Public Library by Asplund, as well as being indebted to Adolf Loos; but this must be rejected in the face of Isozaki's denial of references to other work.

24 See *Architecture and Urbanism*, No 83 (November 1977), pp 15–17, for a comparison between Gunma Prefectural Museum of Modern Art (1970–75) and Richard Meier's Bronx Developmental Centre (1970–77) completed three years later. Isozaki asserted that the two were the products of different intentions and there was no connection between them. He discovered the Meier work after Gunma.

25 'Gunma Prefectural Museum', in *Arata Isozaki, op cit*, p 120.

26 Rudolf Arnheim, *The Power of the Centre: A Study of Composition in the Visual Arts* (London: University of California Press, 1988), pp 56–7.

27 Isozaki gave Bruno Munari's book, *The Discovery of the Square*, as an influence and included both other Western sources as Sol Lewitt and Superstudio as well as traditional Japanese architecture and *furoshiki* (wrapping). He contends that the square is deeply implicated in traditional Japanese architectural tradition, more so than in the West, and identified this with *tateokoshi* method of plan drawing. See Arata Isozaki, 'The Metaphor of the Cube', *Japan Architect, op cit*, p 27.

28 *Ibid*, p 30.

29 *Ibid*, p 30.

30 See Arata Isozaki, 'The Space of Darkness', in *Arata Isozaki, op cit*, pp 53–59. Frampton commented that Isozaki's 'twilight gloom' is the modern parallel of Oriental darkness, something which is absent yet latent within Japanese tradition, p 14.

31 Peregrine Hodson, *A Circle Round the Sun: A Profile of a Foreigner in Japan* (London: Mandarin, 1993), p 226.

32 Arnold Hauser, *Mannerism: The Crisis of the Renaissance and the Origin of Modern Art* (London: Routledge and Kegan Paul, 1965), p 120.

33 *Ibid*, p 294.

34 *Idem*.

35 See Arata Isozaki, 'The Space of Darkness', *op cit*, pp 54–55.

36 *Ibid*, p 53.

37 Kenneth Frampton, 'Post-Metabolism and the Dissolution of Architecture', *op cit*, p 108.

38 See Ian Stewart and Martin Golubitsky, *Fearful Symmetry: Is God a Geometer?* (London: Blackwell, 1992), Ch 2: 'What is Symmetry?'

39 See Stewart and Golubitsky, *ibid*, p 5.

Bibliography

Books

Bognar, Botond, *Contemporary Japanese Architecture: Its Development and Challenge* (New York: Van Nostrand Reinhold, 1985), pp 178–9, 183

Dal Co, Francesco, *Arata Isozaki: Opere e progetti* (Milan: Electa, 1994), pp 48–53

Drew, Philip, *The Architecture of Arata Isozaki* (New York: Harper & Row, 1982), pp 81–86, 113–18

Frampton, Kenneth, *Arata Isozaki, Vol 1, 1959–1978 GA Architect*, No 6 (Tokyo, ADA Edita, 1991), pp 116–133

Ishii, Kazuhiro, *Arata Isozaki, Vol 1* (Tokyo: Space Design, 1977), pp 56–83

Koshalek, Richard, *Arata Isozaki, Architecture 1960–1990* (New York: Rizzoli, 1991), pp 88–97

Ross, Michael Franklin, *Beyond Metabolism: The New Japanese Architecture* (New York: Architectural Record Books, 1978), pp 142–146, 148

Stewart, David B, *The Making of a Modern Japanese Architecture, 1868 to the Present* (Tokyo: Kodansha International, 1987), pp 252–256

Stewart, David B (ed), *Arata Isozaki, 1960–1990 Architecture* (Tokyo: exhibition catalogue, 1991), pp 147–153

Articles
(In chronological order)

'Project of Gunma Modern Art Museum', *Architecture and Urbanism*, Vol 2, No 1 (January 1972), pp 28–31

'Against Architecture, Note III', *Kenchiku-Bunka*, No 12 (December 1972)

'74 Retrospective', *Asahi* newspaper (17 December 1974)

The Display Journal, No 17 (25 December 1974)

'About the Cube: Three-dimensional Aspects', *Shin-Kenchiku* (January 1975), pp 167–200

'Against Architecture, Note IV', *Kenchiku-Bunka*, No 1 (January 1975)

'Arata Isozaki and Descartes' Principles', *Kindai-Kenchiku* (January 1975)

'Museum as a Cave', *Même* (Spring 1975)

Adolpho Natalini, 'Collage Essay on Isozaki's Museum', *Japan Interior Design* (June 1975), pp 21–28 'Gunma Prefectural Museum of Fine Arts', *Japan Interior Design* (June 1975), pp 33–45,

'Two Museums in Japan: Gunma Museum', *Domus*, No 555 (February 1976), pp 14–20

Arata Isozaki, 'Personal Notes on the Cube', *Japan Architect*, Vol 51, No 3 (March 1976), pp 24–6

Charles Jencks, 'Isozaki's Paradoxical Cube', *Japan Architect*, Vol 51, No 3 (March 1976), pp 27–46

Koji Taki, 'World in a Mirror', *Japan Architect*, Vol 51, No 3 (March 1976), pp 73–78, and Vol 51, No 4 (April 1976), pp 68–72

'Gunma Prefectural Museum of Fine Art, 1970–74', *Space Design*, Special Issue, No 140 (April 1976), pp 56–83

'Annual Prize, Architectural Institute of Japan', *Kenchiku-Zashi*, No 8 (August 1976)

Jennifer Taylor, 'The Unreal Architecture of Arata Isozaki', *Progressive Architecture* (September 1976), pp 72–83

'La Metaphore du Cube', and 'Musée d'Art Moderne Takasaki, Japon', *Architecture* (April 1977), pp 58–63

Peter Cook, 'Peter Cook on Arata Isozaki', *Architectural Design*, Vol 47, No 1 (1977), pp 32–37

Bijutsu-Kan [Museum], Sakae Hasegawa (ed), (Tokyo: Graphic-sha, August 1977)

Arata Isozaki, 'A Comparative Study: Bronx Developmental Centre and Gumma Museum of Modern Art,' *Architecture and Urbanism*, No 84 (November 1977), pp 15–17

Arata Isozaki, 'Post-modern Classicism', *Architectural Design*, No 5+6 (May/June 1980), p 86

La Biennale di Venezia, Venice: catalogue, (1980), p 194

Gunma Prefectural Museum of Fine Arts, in *City Segments* (Minneapolis, Minn: Walker Art Centre, 1980)

'Japon Decada del '70', *Summarios* (1981), pp 110–113

Martin Filler, 'Iso-morphisms', *Art in America*, No 2 (1981), pp 117–125

Martin Filler, 'The Art of Isozaki', *House and Garden* (October 1983)

Kurt Andersen, 'Japanese Design: The Golden Age', *Time Australia* magazine, Vol 2, No 38 (17 September 1987), pp 56– 63

John Haycock, 'The Building Blocks of Japanese Architecture', *The Japan Times* (15 April 1989), p 16

Interview with Arata Isozaki, *Gallop* (PR magazine of the Gunma Prefectural Government), (May 1995)

Chronology

January 1971 Arata Isozaki & Associates involved in early schematic design of Gunma-no-mori Park

30 June 1971 1st series: four schemes A, B, C, D adumbrated, range from dispersed to compact layouts

October–December 1971 2nd series sketch designs, further development of four types. Solution emerges in SD 2–3 in December

28 December 1971 3rd series: three schemes refined; east wing expressed as paired rows of cubes

21 January 1972 4th series: three variations, the overall planning is now agreed. Second set of two schemes investigate planning detail

28 March Design Report presented with elevations and plans

September 1972 completion of design phase

October 1972 work begins on site

16 March 1973 footings completed, start on concrete formwork

21 June 1973 scaffolding for reinforced concrete floors and columns

1 September 1973 Temporary Exhibitions hall steel frame erected

20 October 1973 roof completed

March 1974 completion of building work

June–August 1993 design period of new Phase II theatre and restaurant renovation

January–September 1994 construction of theatre and restaurant

Architects, consultants, contractors and suppliers

Location Gunma-no-mori, Iwahana-cho, Takasaki, Gunma Prefecture

Client Gunma Prefectural Government

Architect Arata Isozaki & Associates

Design team Syuichi Fujie, Hiroshi Nishioka

Structural engineers Mamoru Kawaguchi & Engineers Co, Ltd

Mechanical engineers Nippon Kankyo Giken Co, Ltd

Electrical engineers Setsubi Keikaku Co, Ltd

Tea house Sotoji Nakamura

General contractor Inoue Kogyo Co, Ltd

Area of site 258,689 sq m (2,784,5000 sq ft)

Total floor area 7,967 sq m (85,850 sq ft)

Structure reinforced concrete, steel construction

1994 restaurant and theatre:
Architects Arata Isozaki & Associates: Syuichi Fujie, Yasuyuki Watanabe, Shiko Nakamori & Associates: Shiko Nakamori, Tadao Sakamoto

Structural engineers Yanagisawa Structural Engineers: Toshio Yanagisawa

Electrical engineers Yoshida Design Studio: Arimura Yoshida

Mechanical engineers Kankyo Engineering: Keisuke Tanaka

Sculpture Aiko Miyawaki Studio: Aiko Miyawaki, Norishige Matsushita

Furniture Fujie Kazuko Atelier: Kazuo Fujie, Yasuhiro Yoshitake

Sign Ikko Tanaka Design Studio

Lighting Lighting Planners Associates: Kaoru Mende, Hiroshi Inaba

Subcontractors

Piling Ishida Material Industry Co, Ltd

Steel reinforcement Komatsu Steel Co, Ltd

Structural steel work Yoshida Steel Co, Ltd

Concrete Takasaki Concrete Co, Ltd

Formwork Kawakami Co, Ltd

Construction work Sakaguchi Co, Ltd

Elevator installation Tokyo Hydro Industry Co, Ltd

Door sashes Sankyo Aluminium Industry Co, Ltd

Aluminium and panel cladding work Sankyo Aluminium Industry Co, Ltd

Shutter work Susuki Shutter Industry Co, Ltd

Blind work Mitsui Industry Co, Ltd

Stone masonry Sekigahara Stone Co, Ltd; Nakaya Co, Ltd

Glazing work Nakaya Co, Ltd

1994 restaurant and theatre:
Aluminium and panel cladding work Tostem Corporation (theatre); Tajima Jyunzo Ltd (restaurant)

Plaster work Kenji Morita and Machida Kogyo

Marble work Ando marble

Suppliers

Blind work Nichibei Blind

Waterproofing Nisshin Industry Co, Ltd

Glass Nihon Sheet Glass

1994 restaurant and theatre:
Waterproofing Tajima Roofing Co, Ltd

Carpet Kawashima Textile Manufacturers, Ltd

Awards

1975 Annual Prize, Architectural Institute of Japan